Newman's Own

Cookbook

Paul Newman
and A. E. Hotchner

with the culinary and editorial assistance of
Lisa Stalvey and Evie Righter

Simon & Schuster

SIMON & SCHUSTER
Rockefeller Center
1230 Avenue of the Americas
New York, NY 10020

SIMON & SCHUSTER and colophon are registered trademarks
of Simon & Schuster Inc.

Designed by Richard Oriolo

Photos by Janet Durrans appear on pages 22, 42, 68, 72, 79,
113, 145, 158, 201, and 203.

Manufactured in the United States of America

10   9   8   7   6   5   4   3   2   1

Library of Congress Cataloging-in-Publication Data

Newman, Paul.
  Newman's own cookbook / Paul Newman and
A. E. Hotchner ; with the culinary and editorial
assistance of Lisa Stalvey and Evie Righter.
    p.   cm.
  Includes index.
  1. Cookery.   I. Hotchner, A. E.   II. Title.
TX714.N53   1998
641.5—dc21   98-35430
                          CIP

ISBN-10 1-4391-4814-7
ISBN-13 978-1-4391-4814-3

Acknowledgments Newman and Hotchner

cleverly overcame their limited culinary skills by enlisting the invaluable assistance of their editor, Sydny Miner, and Newman's Own food consultant Lisa Stalvey, who contributed her imaginative recipes. The authors are also indebted to food maven and writer Evie Righter.

This book is dedicated to our customers, whose loyalty makes it possible for us to help those who need help.

Contents

Preface

My adult life has been spent in the family of women: my wife, Joanne; five daughters; my housekeeper, Caroline; and a succession of wirehaired terriers, all males who were immediately castrated upon arrival. No wonder I took to wearing an apron by way of disguise, lest I become a capon. What started out as a protective measure became, over time, a stunning discovery of culinary treasures.

These discoveries result from my ability to establish a relationship with the food I'm about to cook. Have you ever had a meaningful conversation with a fillet of scrod? Or a dialogue with a slice of calf's liver?

When I'm about to do some serious cooking, I get ready by putting myself into a self-induced hypnotic trance, much in the same way the Shakirs trance themselves so that they can walk over hot coals and sleep comfortably on a bed of razor-sharp spikes.

Once I'm in my trance, I hold the fillet of scrod in close proximity to my face, and I listen to it. The first sound I hear is that of a popping cork, then the faint sound of cows mooing, and finally the crackling sound of fire. The popping cork leads me to white wine, the moo-cows denote butter, and the roaring fire suggests black basil, all of which I use for my scrod dish (page 104). Over the years I've had several conversations with scrod, and although there may have been a few variations (a ticking clock obviously indicated thyme), for the most part the scrod always had the same things to say to me.

My cooking method becomes more difficult when I cook at somebody else's house—a brisket of beef, say—because my host and hostess constantly interrupt my trance by offering me a Bloody Mary or a slice of local pâté. It's hard enough to get a brisket of beef to speak up without having to politely reject booze and hors d'oeuvres in the process.

Many of the recipes in this book are the result of animated conversations with fish, fowl, fauna, and flora. You may be a bit skeptical of my method—as have been many before you—but to all those snicklers, snipers, and sniders I can only say that after the plates, knives, forks, napkins, and tablecloths were licked clean, nobody ever quarreled with the mystical, magical results of this intimate relationship between the chef and his victuals.

—PAUL NEWMAN

Introduction

I have been asked many times how Paul Newman, who knows a great deal about acting but very little about business, and I, a writer who knows even less, became tycoons—and in the food business yet, as competitive and cutthroat an industry as you can find in Dun & Bradstreet.

The answer is: We did everything wrong. We did just the opposite of what the experts told us to do. Actually, we started with virtually no capital in the bank—a couple of bumbling amateurs trying to fish with no bait in a sea of sharks. It is one thing to want to put a bottle of salad dressing on supermarket shelves but quite another to get it there, and to that end Paul and I consulted a bevy of food experts. We met with the top people of a big marketing company; they advised us to invest a half-million dollars and test the product in "key" shopping plazas all around the United States. "We test-market for Campbell's, Libby, Heinz, and all the biggies," they told us, "and that's how all of them handle a new product." Another big food executive told us that the salad dressing competition was so keen our only chance was to sell our bottles by mail order. And then there was the financial consultant, his desk covered with statistical charts and summaries, who informed us convincingly that we should be prepared to lose $1 million in the first year of operation.

We digested all this, and Newman spoke my mind: "Hotch," he said, "I'll tell you what. Let's test-market it by inviting some of our friends to come over and sample it along with the dressings of all our competitors, using unmarked dishes. If we beat the others, then let's fly right in the teeth of the competition and try to get it on the super-market shelves. To hell with mail order. And I think we should put up forty thousand dollars instead of a million—how about it?"

We shook on it and set up a corporation that we originally called Salad King, with Newman as president and me as vice president and treasurer. Now, before I go any

Newman and Hotchner at work

further, I suppose I had better fill you in on how we got involved with salad dressing in the first place. As long as I can remember, Newman has been rejecting so-called house dressings and concocting his own mix. Captains, maître d's, and sometimes the restaurant owners themselves would scurry around to assemble Newman's ingredients. When we first ate at Elaine's, one of New York's "in" restaurants, virtually all the waiters and Elaine herself gathered around as Paul blended and tasted the ingredients that had been brought to him from the kitchen.

I have watched this scene repeated in a Greek diner, at a wedding party, and in various restaurants from coast to coast. When his kids went off to school, they would ask him to fill a couple of bottles of the salad dressing for them to take along.

All well and good until that day when Paul came over one afternoon to watch a football game and said, "I have a neat idea for Christmas presents. I'm going to give all my friends bottles of my salad dressing. They're always asking me for the recipe, so I'll fill up all the empty wine bottles I've been saving and play Santa Claus. Good idea, huh?"

"Great. They'll love it," I said naively.

"When can we start?"

"Start what?"

"Making the dressing. I figure you and I can do it in an afternoon. How about tomorrow?"

As devious as Tom Sawyer, he is. It took us eight hours of steady labor to mix it, bottle it, cork it, and wrap it. But Newman's friends were delighted, and it was a ritual Paul and I followed every Christmas after that, each year taking longer than the year before, as the list of requests for "Newman's Own Salad Dressing" grew longer and longer.

But finally my sagging back cracked under the mounting pressure. It was the year that it took us three days of sweatshop labor down in Newman's cellar to turn out enough bottles to satisfy his list, by then three pages long. At the end of the third day, Paul stood in the center of the cellar surrounded by all those filled bottles and suggested that we do an extra one hundred bottles and put them up for sale in local food stores.

"You can't stand the thought that on Christmas Day there will be people around here eating salad without your dressing on it, that it?"

He nodded. "How can we be so selfish? Spread good cheer, I say. What's a few more days of bottling?"

I didn't tell him. Instead I said, "It's against the law."

"What is? There is absolutely nothing in my dressing that's illegal."

"The Pure Food Law. You have to have certain certificates."

"Okay, let's look into it."

That was how it started, innocently enough, but over the next several months Newman was driven by his desire to market his dressing. Scarcely a day passed without Paul's calling from some unlikely place to discuss a newly discovered source for the perfect olive oil, the perfect red wine vinegar, or the perfect mustard that he constantly sought. He phoned me from racetracks in between races, from mobile dressing rooms while shooting *Absence of Malice* and *The Verdict*, and from airports on his way to make speeches on behalf of the nuclear freeze movement.

That's when I said, "Listen, Paul, we've been friends for forty-odd years [some of them *really* odd], and I wonder why you're so fixed on marketing your dressing. I ask you, would Clark Gable sell salad dressing? Would Tyrone Power? Humphrey Bogart? Isn't it a little tacky?"

"It's all-natural," Newman said, a touch of pique in his tone. "Just look at the labels on all these other dressings—full of gums, preservatives, chemical additives. That's why. And there's something else."

"What?"

"If we are successful—"

"Yes?"

"I'll tell you then."

So we started operations by finding a modest marketing company in Port Washington, New York, to sell our product, an obscure bottler in Boston to bottle it, and with a total of $40,000 as the entire capital of Salad King, Inc., we set up our headquarters in a little office in Westport, Connecticut, that we furnished with Paul's poolside furniture; in fact, our desk still has a beach umbrella over it. We do not advertise (until this day we haven't spent a penny on advertising), but within a month after our first bottle of Newman's Own had reached the shelves, we had repaid the $40,000 and the orders were rolling in.

It was at the end of our first year of operation, poised by then to introduce a second product—Newman's Own Industrial Strength Marinara Sauce—that Paul said, "We have made nine hundred and twenty thousand dollars in profit, and it's tacky for an actor and a writer to be making money in the food business. So let's give it all away to them what needs it."

That was fifteen years ago, and in those fifteen years we have sold 216,262,680 bottles of Newman's Own oil and vinegar salad dressing; 149,531,280 jars of pasta sauce; 3,278,497,493 portions of popcorn; 37,142,909 jars of salsa; and 81,650,032 pints of lemonade, amounting to $710 million in gross sales. Our total profit from these products to date has been approximately $100 million, every penny of which has been given to deserving charities—a total of 6,088 contributions. We are told that we are the only corporation in the world that gives away all of its profits and starts with zero dollars in the bank on the first of each fiscal year.

So what started out as a lark has become, to our everlasting amazement, a virtual food empire. We have ten factories in the United States and our own trucking network. We are widely distributed in such faraway places as Australia, Japan, Greenland, Puerto Rico, Guam, and England.

"In the beginning," Paul has said, "we were pretty bewildered, trying to decide which among the vast number of deserving charities we should give to. But by now we've developed a pretty good concept—concentrating on organizations for the very young and the very old. But these profits also give me a chance to repay those places that helped me when I needed them: Kenyon University, where I went to school and which whet my appetite for the stage; Yale University drama school, which firmed my resolve to be an actor; the Neighborhood Playhouse and the Actors Studio in New York, where marvelous theater people taught me and encouraged me and put me on the track to a career. It's a kick to be able to give these places solid grants of money so that they can help other young people as they helped me.

"Of course, most of our donations go to major charities, such as Sloan Kettering Cancer Research, Lahey Clinic, New York Foundling Hospital, Cystic Fibrosis, Society to Advance the Retarded, Harlem Restoration, and the American Foundation for AIDS Research, but the biggest kick Hotch and I get is when we can help little obscure organizations that couldn't generate the publicity to attract the attention of big donors."

For example, in 1984 we received this letter written by Sister Carol Putnam, a Sacred Heart nun who ran the Hope Rural School in Indiantown, Florida. "I am hurting desperately for help for a new bus. Ours does not pass inspection for the fall. A new bus costs $26,000. I have written to several sources and have gotten a 'no' so far. A bus will last us ten years and we cannot pick up the children without one."

We phoned Sister Carol and discovered that Hope Rural, which is a school for the children of migrant farmworkers, might have to go out of existence because its fourteen-year-old secondhand school bus had been condemned.

Prior to the founding of the Hope Rural School, the children had been denied any consistent schooling. They were prevented from attending regular classes by the wretched poverty that forced their farmworker families to travel constantly throughout the country in search of seasonal work. The youngsters often labored in the fields alongside their parents, returning to central Florida every winter to harvest the state's citrus crops; when times got particularly hard, these families slept under bridges and in abandoned cars. Many of the children had never held a schoolbook or heard a nursery rhyme until the Hope Rural School, built by the migrant workers themselves, began a flexible term that allowed the children to attend classes during the picking season without having to enroll in a normal September-to-June school year.

"But when our school bus was condemned this past summer by the state authorities, my worst fears were realized," Sister Carol told us. "With no bus to transport these children from their homes miles away, the school would be worthless, and many of the children would return to their hopeless lives in the fields."

Sister Carol said she had taken $1,000 that had been earmarked for teachers' salaries and put a down payment on a new school bus, hoping that somehow, some way, someone would donate money for the bus. The sisters at Hope Rural had written to foundations and called wealthy men and women from the nearby Palm Beach area, but the school could find no one willing to help. And then, the day before our phone call, as time and hope were running out, tragedy almost struck.

It was a blisteringly hot November afternoon, and the condemned school bus was making its way along back roads to bring a handful of students home for the day. As the bus approached the flashing lights of a railroad crossing, the driver applied the brakes, but the brakes wouldn't hold and the bus continued on toward the tracks. Warning whistles blared the approach of the Amtrack express from Tampa, but with no time to get the children out, the driver decided to floor the gas pedal, charging across the tracks moments before the train swept by.

The very day that we spoke with Sister Carol, our check for the immediate delivery of a new bus to Hope Rural was on its way to the Blue Bird Bus Company.

In 1997, after thirteen years of hard use, the nuns of Hope Rural informed us that the bus had worn out, and we happily sent them a replacement.

We have a substantial Canadian market, and we annually donate all our Canadian profits to three charities there: the Hospital for Sick Children, the St. Boniface General Hospital Research Foundation, and the Famous People Players, a remarkable nonprofit group of black light puppeteers who have performed all over the world, most recently in China. Ten of the thirteen members of the troupe are mentally handicapped.

As we do with Canada, we also return to Australian and British charities (we have factories in both countries) the substantial profits that we realize from the sale of our products there and in every foreign country where we do business. At present we make donations to charities in Africa, Argentina, Australia, Bolivia, Bosnia, Brazil, Cambodia, Canada, Croatia, Czechoslovakia, Denmark, El Salvador, France, Germany,

Haiti, Hong Kong, Iceland, Ireland, Israel, Japan, Korea, New Zealand, Russia, Sweden, Switzerland, United Kingdom, and Vietnam.

Newman and I have always had a lively and inquisitive interest in food, as the recipes in this book will attest. We have recommended the use of our high-quality products, but certainly you can replace our stuff with other brands if you prefer. The recipes themselves come from three sources:

1. Some are our own favorites, invented by us, while others are contributions from family and friends.

2. Some are recipes that won the contest that we sponsor every year in conjunction with *Good Housekeeping* magazine. The contest awards cash prizes to the winners' designated charities. There are special contest categories for children and for professional food critics.

3. Some were concocted for us by a young chef named Lisa Stalvey, whom we met when Paul and I regularly dined at her restaurant in Santa Monica while Newman was filming his movie *Twilight*.

As for Newman's personal recipes, you will find that the dishes he cooks have his own characteristics—simple, straightforward, good quality, just enough seasoning to be exciting but not overwhelming, with an unexpected flair, a touch of the exotic. Even his hamburger. Really. Give it a try.

—A. E. HOTCHNER

It's our belief that eating well is the best revenge, and the recipes collected herein have been chosen with that in mind. These are our favorite recipes and those of our families and friends.

Our guidelines were that the dishes be simple, imaginative, and digestible. Don't expect to find exotic game birds floating in a cream and brandy sauce or lobster stuffed with caviar and foie gras.

These are the kind of wholesome, tasty dishes that would bring joy to the hearts of Butch Cassidy and Ernest Hemingway if the two of them happened to have dinner together.

—PAUL NEWMAN AND A. E. HOTCHNER

Starters

Paul Newman's Tomato and Endive Salad ▪ Tomato, Onion, and Goat Cheese Salad ▪ Paul's Caesar Salad ▪ Avocado and Feta Cheese with Lemon-Cumin Dressing ▪ Scallop and Shrimp Salad with Shanghai Citrus Dressing ▪ Newman's Vinaigrette Dressing ▪ Fat-Free Sweet-Tart Mustard Dressing ▪ Cheese Puffs with Salsa Cream Filling ▪ Holly Hunter's Zucchini Pancakes with Smoked Salmon and Yogurt-Dill Sauce ▪ Grilled Scallops with Avocado Cream and Salsa

I have two favorite appetizers. One is a dozen littleneck clams on the half-shell, topped with a squirt of lemon juice. The other one I've forgotten, but it probably has something to do with celery and/or beer.

I like any kind of melon as a starter, even watermelon, although melon is better eaten in the sauna or the shower, which makes me wonder whether it's an appetizer or a washcloth.

—PAUL NEWMAN

Newman as King Beer, Whoopi Goldberg as his queen, performing in the 1996 gala at the Hole in the Wall Gang Camp

Some people have sexual dreams, but I dream about salad. Then when I wake up, I want to eat the salad I dreamed about. (This morning I didn't eat anything because I dreamed about liver last night, and I hate liver.)

My salad dressing is literally something I dreamed up, the main part of it during a long night's sleep; the adjustments came in short afternoon naps.

—PAUL NEWMAN

Paul Newman's Tomato and Endive Salad

I like salads for lunch, and this one is at the top of my list. Of course, I use Newman's Own dressing on them, but if you have the questionable taste of preferring some others, suit yourself. ■ SERVES 4

2 large, ripe fresh tomatoes

8 ounces endive (about 3 medium)

3 slices bacon

Newman's Own salad dressing or Vinaigrette Dressing (page 30)

Cut the tomatoes into small dice. Slice the endive to make 4 equal portions and mix with the tomatoes. Cook the bacon until very crisp. Crumble and then sprinkle over the salad. Toss with salad dressing to taste.

Tomato, Onion, and Goat Cheese Salad

If butterleaf lettuce is not available in your market, use red leaf or Boston lettuce here. Soft-leafed lettuce of any kind is the way to go. Avoid anything too crunchy. ■ SERVES 6 TO 8 AS A STARTER

3 heads butterleaf lettuce, leaves separated and 6 large outer leaves reserved for use as cups

2 heads radicchio, cut into julienne strips

3 vine-ripened tomatoes, cored and cut into quarters

½ cup finely chopped yellow onion

1 small log (4 ounces) unashed goat cheese, crumbled

⅓ to ½ cup Newman's Own Balsamic Vinaigrette or your favorite

In a large salad bowl, combine the lettuces (not including the leaves reserved for cups), tomatoes, onion, and goat cheese. Add the dressing, beginning with ⅓ cup and using up to ½ cup if you like, and toss.

To serve, place a lettuce cup on each salad plate, then arrange the salad in and around it. Divide the tomatoes and goat cheese evenly.

Paul's Caesar Salad

There's no raw egg in the dressing here! Classic or not, this is a mighty fine Caesar salad. If you're in a hurry, use prepackaged romaine hearts; they usually come three to a package. You'll need two packages. Do take the time to make your own croutons, though. They make a certifiable difference, as do great tomatoes (even if they are a nontraditional ingredient). ■ SERVES 6

CROUTONS

½ sourdough baguette, sliced into 6 rounds about 1½ inches thick

1 stick (8 tablespoons) unsalted butter, melted

2 tablespoons chopped garlic

SALAD

2 heads romaine lettuce, torn into bite-sized pieces, or 2 packages romaine hearts

½ to ¾ cup Newman's Own Caesar Dressing or your favorite

2 large, ripe beefsteak tomatoes, cored and cut into 6 slices each

¾ cup freshly grated, shaved, or thinly sliced Parmesan cheese

To make the croutons: Dip each piece of bread into the melted butter. In a medium skillet, combine the remaining butter with the garlic and heat until foamy. Add the bread rounds in 1 layer and brown lightly on both sides in the garlic butter, about 1 minute per side. Remove and reserve.

Toss the romaine pieces in a bowl with about ¼ cup of the dressing. Arrange the lettuce on plates and add 2 tomato slices and 1 crouton per serving. Sprinkle with cheese or lay the shavings or slices on top. Serve the remaining dressing on the side.

Avocado and Feta Cheese with Lemon-Cumin Dressing

Don't be put off by what looks like large amounts of both vinegar and lemon juice in this dressing. The dressing *is* tangy, but it's great with this salad in particular and almost any other green salad as well. You will have quite a bit left over. It keeps for several weeks, covered, in the refrigerator.

You'll have half an avocado left over. We suggest eating it right on the spot. If that seems overly aggressive, there's always the option of rubbing it with lemon juice, wrapping it airtight, and hiding it in the refrigerator. ■ MAKES ABOUT 1½ CUPS OF DRESSING ■ SERVES 6

LEMON-CUMIN DRESSING

½ cup sherry vinegar

¼ cup fresh lemon juice

1 teaspoon Pommery (French whole-grain) mustard

¼ teaspoon chopped garlic

2 teaspoons ground cumin

½ teaspoon salt

1 teaspoon freshly ground black pepper

¾ cup extra-virgin olive oil

SALAD

4 small heads romaine, outer leaves removed and discarded, inner leaves cut into julienne strips

5 Roma tomatoes, chopped

½ small red onion, chopped

1 cup crumbled feta cheese

2 avocados

To make the lemon-cumin dressing: Place all the ingredients except the oil in a blender and blend on high until combined. With the blender on "stir," add the oil in a slow, steady stream and blend for about 15 seconds, until combined.

To make the salad: Combine all the ingredients in a large bowl except the avocados. Toss with about ⅓ cup of the dressing, adding more to taste if desired. Divide the salad among 6 salad plates.

Peel, pit, and quarter the avocados, then cut each quarter, leaving it attached at the top, into thin slices. "Fan" the avocado slices, spreading them carefully on one side of each plate. (If you prefer, you can chop the avocados and add an equal amount to each salad.) Pour some of the remaining dressing into a bowl to spoon over the avocado.

Scallop and Shrimp Salad with Shanghai Citrus Dressing

You'll have Shanghai citrus dressing left over after you make this salad. It shouldn't be a problem, though, because it is terrific as a basting sauce for grilled fish or shellfish. It is also excellent on Chinese chicken salad or on something as simple as plain roasted or grilled vegetables.

■ SERVES 6

SHANGHAI CITRUS DRESSING

¼ cup soy sauce

¼ cup fresh orange juice

⅓ cup seasoned rice wine vinegar

2 tablespoons Dijon mustard

1 tablespoon honey

½ cup olive oil

¼ teaspoon salt

1 teaspoon freshly ground black pepper

SEAFOOD

12 sea scallops

6 large shrimp, peeled and deveined

4 tablespoons olive oil

salt and freshly ground black pepper to taste

VEGETABLES

24 thin asparagus spears, ends trimmed and peeled

5 cups mixed baby greens

1 hothouse cucumber, diced

½ small red onion, thinly sliced

1 tablespoon finely chopped cilantro

To make the dressing: In a large bowl, combine the soy sauce, orange juice, vinegar, mustard, and honey. Whisk together well. Add the oil in a slow, steady stream, whisking until fully incorporated. Whisk in the salt and pepper.

Prepare the seafood: Combine the scallops, shrimp, 2 tablespoons of the oil, salt, and pepper in a bowl. Set aside at room temperature.

Prepare the vegetables: Bring a large skillet of salted water to a rolling boil, add the asparagus spears, and blanch for 1 minute. Remove with a slotted spatula to a wide, shallow pan filled with ice water to stop the cooking and set the color. Remove when cool and pat dry with paper towels. Chop the spears and combine with the baby greens, cucumber, and onion in a large bowl.

To finish the seafood: Heat 1 tablespoon of the remaining oil in a large skillet or sauté pan over medium heat until hot. Add the scallops in 1 layer and cook for 5 minutes. Turn and cook 3 minutes more. Remove to a plate and set aside.

Pour the remaining tablespoon of oil into the pan, add the shrimp, and cook for a total of 5 to 7 minutes, turning, or until just cooked through.

Just before serving, stir the cilantro into the dressing. Toss the salad with about ½ cup of the dressing, then divide among 6 plates. Top each serving with 2 scallops and 1 shrimp. Season with salt and pepper. Serve with some of the remaining dressing to spoon over the shellfish.

Newman's Vinaigrette Dressing

Any oil and vinegar dressing (vinaigrette) can be used in the recipes in this book that call for Newman's Own.

To make a basic vinaigrette, mix 1 part vinegar or lemon juice with 3 parts oil. Season with salt and pepper, and add Dijon mustard to taste. Use extra-virgin olive oil and high-quality white or red wine vinegar for the best results. Vary the ratio of oil to vinegar for a sharper or milder dressing. You may add garlic (chopped or a whole peeled clove for subtle flavoring), dried or fresh herbs, or other seasonings. For variety try an herb vinegar in place of plain wine vinegar.

Fat-Free Sweet-Tart Mustard Dressing The

longer this dressing sits, the better it gets. Besides being fat-free, it is also multipurpose. Use it as a dressing—on baby spinach leaves, for example—as a marinade for fish, poultry, and meat, or as a dipping sauce. We've made a lot of it because you'll use a lot of it. It is not a recipe that should be made in smaller amounts; the flavor doesn't hold up when the amounts are reduced.

■ MAKES ABOUT 3½ CUPS

1 cup Pommery (French whole-grain) mustard

1 cup Dijon mustard

1 cup honey mustard

¼ cup balsamic vinegar

1 tablespoon soy sauce

1 tablespoon fresh lemon juice

1 tablespoon fresh orange juice

1 teaspoon pure maple syrup

½ teaspoon salt

1 teaspoon freshly ground black pepper

Combine all the ingredients in a large jar or container with a lid. Stir together well until completely combined. Cover the jar and store it in the refrigerator. For best results, let stand 1 day in the refrigerator before using. Stir or shake before using.

The dressing will keep, covered and chilled, for 1 month.

Cheese Puffs with Salsa Cream Filling

These puffs are made with choux pastry, the same dough that is used for the great French dessert, eclairs. Unlike some French doughs, it is not hard to prepare, and is you want to make this really easy for yourself, bake the puffs in advance and freeze them. Defrost at room temperature and fill just before serving.

■ **MAKES 36 PUFFS**

DOUGH

6 tablespoons unsalted butter, cut into
    pieces

1 teaspoon salt

freshly ground black pepper to taste

freshly grated nutmeg to taste
    (optional)

1 cup flour

4 large eggs plus 1 egg, lightly beaten,
    for the egg wash

1 cup plus 3 tablespoons finely grated
    cheddar or Swiss cheese

FILLING

one 11-ounce jar Newman's Own All-
    Natural Bandito Salsa or your
    favorite

8 ounces whipped cream cheese

Preheat the oven to 425°F. Grease 2 baking sheets.

To make the dough: In a heavy 2-quart saucepan, combine 1 cup of water with the butter, salt, pepper, and nutmeg. When the butter has melted and the water is boiling, remove the pan from the heat and beat in the flour all at once with a wooden spoon. Stir vigorously until the mixture forms a ball and leaves the sides of the pan. (If it does not, return the pan to medium heat and beat vigorously for 1 to 2 minutes, until it forms a ball.) Off of the heat, beat in the 4 eggs, 1 at a time, until each is thoroughly incorporated. Beat in the 1 cup of grated cheese.

Transfer the dough to a pastry bag fitted with a plain ½-inch tip. Pipe rounds on the prepared baking sheets, each about 1 inch in diameter, 1 inch high, and 2 inches apart. With a pastry brush, very carefully brush the tops of the rounds with some of the egg wash, being sure not to let any drip onto the baking sheets. (It will act like glue and prevent the puffs from puffing.) Sprinkle the remaining cheese over the tops of the rounds.

Bake for 20 to 25 minutes, or until golden and crisp. Remove from the oven and turn off the oven. With the tip of a small, sharp knife, pierce the top side of each puff, then return the baking sheets to the oven to dry for 10 minutes. Remove and let cool on wire racks.

While the puffs are baking or as they cool, make the filling: Drain the salsa. In a bowl, combine the cream cheese with half of the drained salsa. Depending on how much of a salsa flavor you like, continue to add salsa to taste, blending it in well.

With a small, sharp knife, cut off the top half of the puffs. Spoon filling into each puff and place the tops of the puffs rakishly back on.

Holly Hunter's Zucchini Pancakes with Smoked Salmon and Yogurt-Dill Sauce

These are elegant and beautiful and make a great first course or entree for brunch. You can also quarter the finished pancakes and serve them as an appetizer. Don't stint on the quality of smoked salmon. This is a case where more is more.

■ SERVES 6

YOGURT-DILL SAUCE

1 cup plain low-fat yogurt
¼ cup finely chopped fresh dill
salt and freshly ground black pepper to taste
juice of 1 lemon

PANCAKES

2 medium zucchini, ends trimmed
2 large Idaho potatoes, scrubbed but not peeled
1 small red onion, thinly sliced and cut into julienne strips
2 tablespoons olive oil
salt and freshly ground black pepper to taste
2 tablespoons vegetable oil for cooking
1½ teaspoons unsalted butter, melted, for cooking

ACCOMPANIMENTS

2 cups mixed baby greens
12 ounces sliced Norwegian smoked salmon or gravlax (2 slices per serving)
½ cup chopped chives for garnish
very thin lemon slices for garnish
freshly ground black pepper to taste

To make the sauce: In a ceramic or plastic bowl, combine all the ingredients, cover, and chill. (If you are making the sauce in advance, add the lemon juice just before serving, or the yogurt will separate.)

To make the pancakes: Grate the zucchini and potatoes on the large-hole side of a hand-held box grater or in a food processor fitted with the shredding disk. Put the grated vegetables in a bowl and add the onion, olive oil, salt, and pepper.

Preheat the oven to 300°F. In a 7½-inch nonstick omelet pan, heat 1 teaspoon of the vegetable oil together with ¼ teaspoon of the melted butter over medium-high heat until hot. Pour ¾ cup of the grated vegetables and spread the mixture to the edges of the pan, pressing down firmly with a rubber spatula, to form a pancake about ¼ inch thick. Cook about 3 minutes, until the edges begin to brown. Gently lift the pancake with the spatula, to check the underside. If it is deep golden brown in color, turn (or flip) the pancake and cook 3 to 4 minutes more, until golden. Remove the pancake to a paper-towel-lined plate to drain, then transfer to a baking sheet. Place in the oven to keep warm.

Make pancakes with the remaining ingredients in the same manner, being sure to add 1 teaspoon of oil and a bit of butter to the pan before making a new pancake.

To serve, put a generous ¼ cup of greens on each of 6 salad plates. Spread each pancake with about 2 tablespoons (or more to taste) of yogurt-dill sauce, then put a pancake on each plate on the greens. Arrange 2 slices of salmon on top of each pancake. Garnish each serving with some chives, several lemon slices, and a generous grinding of pepper. Serve the remaining sauce in a bowl on the side.

Grilled Scallops with Avocado Cream and Salsa

As anyone who loves seviche knows, fresh lime and seafood were made for each other. Add a few other south-of-the-border ingredients like avocado, cumin, and tortillas, and you have a dynamite dish.

■ MAKES 32 NIBBLES

4 tablespoons olive oil

3 tablespoons fresh lime juice

1½ teaspoons grated lime zest

¾ to 1 teaspoon salt

½ teaspoon ground cumin

¼ teaspoon freshly ground black pepper

32 sea scallops

4 (8-inch) flour tortillas, cut into eighths (32 wedges)

2 firm, ripe avocados

½ cup finely chopped red onion

¼ cup plain low-fat or no-fat yogurt

2 cups shredded iceberg lettuce

¾ cup Newman's Own All-Natural Bandito Salsa or your favorite

In a medium ceramic or glass bowl, whisk together 2 tablespoons of oil, 2 tablespoons of lime juice, ½ teaspoon of grated zest, ¼ teaspoon of salt, cumin, and pepper. Add the scallops and marinate, covered, in the refrigerator for 1 hour.

In a large nonstick skillet, heat the remaining 2 tablespoons of oil over medium-high heat until hot. Add the tortilla wedges in batches and cook until golden brown on both sides, 1 to 2 minutes. Drain the wedges on paper towels.

Peel, pit, and coarsely mash the avocados in another medium bowl. Stir in the onion, yogurt, and the remaining lime juice, zest, and salt.

When ready to serve, preheat the grill or broiler. In a broiler pan, cook the scallops about 3 inches from the heat until cooked through, about 4 to 5 minutes.

To serve, spread 2 teaspoons of avocado cream on each tortilla wedge. Top with 1 tablespoon of lettuce and 1 scallop, and finish with about 1 teaspoon of salsa. Repeat with the remaining ingredients.

Soups, Stews, and Chilies

Matthew Broderick's Tortilla Soup ▪ Nell Newman's Chicken Soup ▪ Nathan Lane's South-of-the-Border Zucchini Soup ▪ Carole King's Sweet Pea Soup with Spicy Cream ▪ Roasted Squash Soup with Port ▪ Nell Newman's Cauliflower and Parmesan Soup with Essence of Lemon ▪ Joanne Woodward's Gazpacho ▪ Melissa Newman's Minestrone ▪ Lima Bean and Red Onion Soup ▪ Judge Roy's Zesty White Bean Bisque ▪ Franklin County, Florida's Own Frankly Fantastic Seafood Gumbo ▪ Towering Inferno Creole Posole ▪ Beef Stew with Potatoes and Pesto ▪ Robert Redford's Lamb Chili with Black Beans ▪ Vegetarian Black Bean Chili

Matthew Broderick's Tortilla Soup

This bold soup with big flavors is not for the lily-livered or faint of heart. We will let you adjust the amount of cumin and cilantro to suit your taste. Cold beer makes a very fine antidote; a crisp salad is a good accompaniment.

■ MAKES ABOUT 8 CUPS ■ SERVES 6

3 large, very ripe tomatoes
¼ cup vegetable oil
¼ cup olive oil
¼ cup whole cloves garlic (about 4 large cloves)
1 medium yellow onion, chopped
1 small jalapeño chili pepper, seeded and ribbed
one 24-ounce can chopped peeled tomatoes
¼ cup chili powder
¼ to ⅓ cup ground cumin, or to taste
1 tablespoon garlic powder

1 cup chopped cilantro (or less, according to taste)
2 bay leaves
6 to 8 cups chicken stock
4 corn tortillas
salt and freshly ground black pepper to taste

GARNISH

unsalted blue or white corn chips, broken up
1 avocado, diced
6 teaspoons sour cream (optional)

Blacken the tomatoes in the vegetable oil in a very hot cast-iron skillet or under the broiler about 4 inches from the heat. Turn with tongs until charred all over. (You can also char them without the oil, speared on the end of a long fork over an open gas burner.) Let cool, then core and halve.

Heat the olive oil in a stockpot over high heat until hot. Add the garlic and onion, cover, and cook over low heat for 3 minutes to soften. Add the jalapeño, canned tomatoes, blackened tomatoes, chili powder, cumin, garlic powder, cilantro, bay leaves, and 6 cups of the chicken stock. Add water to cover the ingredients by about 5 inches and bring to a boil. Lower the heat and simmer the soup for 30 minutes.

While the soup is cooking, blacken the tortillas over an open grill or in a very hot un-oiled cast-iron skillet. Let cool, then break up the tortillas and add them to the soup. Cook for 15 minutes. Remove the bay leaves.

Puree the hot soup in batches in a blender or food processor, filling the container only half full each time. Blend on low, being sure to hold the lid down firmly. Return the soup to the stockpot and thin if necessary with the remaining chicken stock. Season the soup with salt and pepper and heat through.

Serve in bowls, garnished with the corn chips, avocado, and sour cream.

And he asked himself—Good Lord, what have we unleashed?

—PAUL NEWMAN ON SEEING THE FIRST PROFIT AND
LOSS STATEMENT OF NEWMAN'S OWN

Nell Newman's Chicken Soup

My father has an inexhaustible fondness for soups and often makes quick-stop chicken soup with a prepared mix that he combines with noodles and fresh vegetables. In fact, give my father a hearty soup, a can of beer, and a bag of popcorn, and he is as close to heaven as he can get.

He does handstands over my chicken soup, but in all fairness I must acknowledge that my recipe was inspired by the chicken soup our English governess, Duffy, made for us when we were little. ■ SERVES 8 TO 10

STOCK

- 2 tablespoons olive oil
- 2 large leeks, well washed and the white parts chopped
- 3 carrots, sliced into ¼-inch pieces
- 2 stalks celery, coarsely chopped
- 2 medium onions, coarsely chopped
- 4 to 6 cloves garlic, mashed
- 1 cup dry white wine
- ¾ cup minced parsley
- 2 tablespoons minced fresh marjoram
- 1 plump roasting chicken (4 to 5 pounds), cut into quarters, plus 2 thighs

CHICKEN SOUP

- 2 stalks celery, coarsely chopped
- 1 large leek, well washed and white part chopped
- 3 carrots, cut into ¼-inch pieces
- 2 medium onions, coarsely chopped
- 1 cup fresh or frozen peas
- 1 cup fresh or frozen corn
- 1 bay leaf
- ¾ cup minced parsley
- 2 tablespoons minced fresh marjoram
- salt and freshly ground black pepper to taste

- egg noodles

To make the stock: Heat the olive oil in a stockpot until hot. Add the leeks, carrots, celery, onions, and garlic, and cook, stirring, until lightly browned. Add the wine, parsley, marjoram, and 4 quarts of cold water, and bring the mixture to a boil. Add the chicken and simmer for 1 hour. Remove the chicken breasts, let cool, and refrigerate. Continue simmering the stock 3 to 4 hours. Let the stock cool, strain it into a large bowl, and refrigerate.

When ready to serve, skim off all the fat from the stock and bring to a boil. Add all the vegetables and bay leaf. Skin, bone, and dice the breasts. Add to the pot with the parsley and marjoram. (You may want to add additional water at this point to thin the soup.) Finally, season with salt and pepper.

Meanwhile, in a separate pot, cook a generous amount of egg noodles, then drain them.

To serve, place a portion of cooked noodles in each soup bowl and ladle soup over the top. Serve with a crusty baguette or your favorite grilled cheese sandwiches as accompaniments.

Nathan Lane's South-of-the-Border Zucchini Soup

There is no cream in this soup, but it still manages to have a creamy, wonderful texture. Try it with garlic bread and a goat cheese salad for a light lunch or supper. ■ MAKES ABOUT 7 CUPS ■ SERVES 6

¼ cup olive oil

1 bunch scallions, ends trimmed, both green and white parts, and chopped

½ medium red onion, chopped

3 cloves garlic

2 tablespoons ground cumin

3 large or 4 medium zucchini (1½ to 2 pounds), ends trimmed and quartered

1 small white potato, peeled and diced

6 cups vegetable or chicken stock

salt and freshly ground black pepper to taste

½ cup shredded low-fat cheddar cheese for garnish

½ cup shredded low-fat Monterey Jack cheese for garnish

Newman, Nathan Lane, and the Hole in the Wall Gang Camp kids

Heat the olive oil in a large saucepan over high heat until hot but not smoking. Add the scallions, onion, garlic, and cumin, and cook, stirring, for 3 minutes. Add the zucchini, potato, and stock, and bring to a boil. Lower the heat to medium and simmer for 40 minutes.

Puree the hot soup in a blender in batches, filling the container only half full each time. Blend on low and be sure to hold the lid down firmly. Pour the soup back into the saucepan, season with salt and pepper, and reheat.

To serve, ladle the soup into 6 bowls and garnish each serving with a rounded tablespoon each of the cheddar and Monterey Jack cheeses.

Carole King's Sweet Pea Soup with Spicy Cream

If you can't find mascarpone, one of Italy's richest cow's milk cheeses, don't just abandon making the spicy cream garnish; use sour cream instead. The subtle flavor that mascarpone adds makes it worth looking for; some well-stocked gourmet stores and supermarkets carry it.

■ MAKES 6½ CUPS ■ SERVES 6

SPICY CREAM

4 ounces mascarpone cheese

juice of ¼ lemon

¼ teaspoon crushed red pepper flakes

¼ teaspoon freshly ground black
   pepper

pinch of salt

SOUP

2 tablespoons vegetable oil

¼ cup whole cloves garlic

½ medium red onion, chopped

1 small carrot, chopped

1 small red potato, peeled and chopped

two 10-ounce packages frozen baby
   peas, thawed, or 2 pounds fresh
   peas, shelled

6 to 8 cups vegetable or chicken stock

salt and freshly ground black pepper to
   taste

To make the spicy cream: Combine all the ingredients in a small bowl. Cover and refrigerate until ready to use. The cream keeps, covered and chilled, for 2 days.

To make the soup: Heat the oil in a large saucepan or stockpot over high heat until hot. Add the garlic and onion, and cook, stirring, for 5 minutes, or until the garlic is golden. Add the carrot, potato, and peas, and cook, stirring, for 3 minutes. Pour in 6 cups of the stock and bring the mixture to a slow, rolling boil. Turn the heat to low and simmer for 45 minutes.

Puree the soup in a blender in batches, filling the container only half full each time. Blend on low and be sure to hold the lid down firmly. Pour the soup back into the pan and thin it to the desired consistency with additional stock if desired. Season with salt and pepper, and heat through.

Divide the soup among heated bowls and top each serving with a big spoonful of the spicy cream. Serve hot.

Roasted Squash Soup with Port

If you are lucky enough to find banana squash in your market, use it; otherwise, butternut works just fine. This is a good fall soup, filling but not rich—basically a vegetable stock puree. The toasted pumpkin seed garnish adds a lovely contrast of texture and flavor to the silky soup. ■ MAKES ABOUT 8 CUPS ■ SERVES 6

1 butternut squash (4 to 5 pounds), halved and seeded
¼ cup vegetable oil
1 Idaho potato, peeled and chopped
1 yellow onion, chopped
⅓ cup whole cloves garlic (about 6 medium cloves)
6 to 8 cups chicken stock

¼ cup ruby port
½ teaspoon ground allspice
salt and freshly ground black pepper to taste
2 tablespoons unsalted butter
toasted pumpkin seeds for garnish (optional)

Preheat the oven to 450°F.

Brush the cut surfaces of the squash with 2 tablespoons of the oil and bake on a cookie sheet until tender, about 45 minutes. Let cool and scrape out the flesh into a bowl.

Heat the remaining 2 tablespoons of oil in a soup pot over high heat until hot. Add the potato, onion, and garlic, and cook, stirring, for 5 minutes. Add 6 cups of the stock and bring to a boil. Stir in the cooked squash, port, and allspice, and cook at a low simmer for 40 minutes.

Puree the hot soup in a blender in batches, filling the container only half full each time. Blend on low speed and be sure to hold the lid down firmly. Pour the soup back into the pot set over low heat. Add additional stock if necessary to arrive at the desired consistency. Add salt and pepper. Swirl in the butter.

Serve in soup bowls and garnish with the pumpkin seeds.

Nell Newman's Cauliflower and Parmesan Soup with Essence of Lemon

This is a fantastically fresh, slightly lemony soup with new green peas (not canned!) for color. It goes very well with my Sesame Loaves (page 180). This soup originated during one of my refrigerator-cleaning sprees, in which I throw all my leftovers into a pot, heat them, and see what happens. ■ MAKES ABOUT 8 CUPS ■ SERVES 8 TO 10

1 large head cauliflower (2 to 2¼ pounds), cut into 1-inch pieces
1 medium onion, chopped
6 cups chicken or vegetable stock
1 cup uncooked millet

⅓ cup freshly grated Parmesan cheese
juice of ½ lemon
1 cup fresh peas (about 1 pound peas, unshelled)
salt and freshly ground pepper

Place the cauliflower in a pot along with the onion and stock. Simmer over medium heat until tender, about 15 to 20 minutes.

While the cauliflower is cooking, wash the millet in a strainer. Put in another pot along with 2¼ cups of water and cook over medium heat until soft and fluffy. (This may require a bit more water.)

When the cauliflower is cooked, place small batches in a blender or food processor along with the stock. Blend each batch until smooth. Return to the pot set over low heat. Add the cheese, lemon juice, millet, peas, salt, and pepper. Mix well and warm for 5 minutes before serving.

Joanne Woodward's Gazpacho

Don't throw out that leftover salad! Try this refreshing soup instead. You can include lettuce, tomato, cucumber, scallions, onion, bell pepper, and/or radishes.

■ **MAKES ABOUT 5 CUPS** ■ **SERVES 4 TO 6**

2 cups leftover tossed salad with
    vinaigrette dressing
2 cups Newman's Own Sock-It-To-'Em
    Sockarooni Spaghetti Sauce or your
    favorite meatless sauce

1 cup beef bouillon
chopped cucumber, scallion, and
    tomato for garnish (optional)

Puree the salad ingredients, sauce, and bouillon together in a blender or food processor. Add more bouillon if necessary to reach the desired consistency. Refrigerate for 1 hour.

Garnish each serving with the chopped cucumber, scallion, and tomato.

Melissa Newman's Minestrone

This hearty soup makes a meal with some crusty bread and a green salad. You might like some grated cheese sprinkled on top, too. ■ MAKES AT LEAST 6 CUPS ■ SERVES 8

4 ounces dried lima beans or kidney beans, soaked overnight, cooked until tender, and drained

1 large onion, chopped

1 stalk celery, chopped

1 carrot, chopped

¼ head green cabbage, shredded

4 ounces fresh peas

1 or 2 chicken or vegetable bouillon cubes

2 cups Newman's Own Sock-It-To-'Em Sockarooni Spaghetti Sauce or your favorite meatless sauce

Simmer the beans, onion, celery, carrot, cabbage, and peas in 3 cups of water (or more if needed) with the bouillon cubes until the vegetables are tender, about 12 to 15 minutes. Add the sauce and simmer gently 5 minutes more. Serve hot.

Lissie, Paul Newman, and Tony Randall at a Hole in the Wall Gang Camp gala

Lima Bean and Red Onion Soup

If you swore off lima beans a long time ago, try this substantial, flavorful soup and see if it isn't time for some revisionist thinking. Try it with Paul's Caesar Salad (page 26) for a light lunch or supper. This dish uses no dairy products, and there's not too much fat, either, which makes it politically correct, too.

■ **MAKES ABOUT 5½ CUPS** ■ **SERVES 6**

¼ cup vegetable oil

1½ medium red onions, chopped

4 cloves garlic

two 10-ounce packages frozen baby lima beans, thawed

4½ cups chicken stock

salt and freshly ground black pepper to taste

¼ cup chopped chives for garnish

Heat the oil in a large saucepan over high heat until hot. Add the onions and garlic, and cook, stirring, for 5 minutes. Add the lima beans and stock, and cook, stirring occasionally, for 30 minutes.

Puree the hot soup in a blender in batches, filling the container only half full each time. Blend on low speed and be sure to hold the lid down firmly. Pour the soup back into the saucepan, season with salt and pepper, and reheat.

To serve, ladle a scant cup into each soup bowl and garnish with the chives.

Judge Roy's Zesty White Bean Bisque

Paul says, "Here's a recipe that will knock your socks off." Tresa Rabchuk of Locust Valley, New York, adds a new twist to a classic creamy bean soup with the addition of Newman's Own Sock-It-To-'Em Sockarooni Spaghetti Sauce. The 1996 runner-up in the Newman's Own/*Good Housekeeping* Recipe Contest, her award went to the Animal Medical Center. ■ MAKES 8 FIRST-COURSE SERVINGS

1 large onion, chopped

2 tablespoons unsalted butter or margarine

2 cloves garlic, crushed with a garlic press

one 8-ounce slice center-cut ham (about ½ inch thick), already cooked, diced

two 15- to 19-ounce cans white kidney beans, rinsed and drained

two 11-ounce cans whole kernel corn, drained

2 cups half-and-half or light cream

1 cup Newman's Own Sock-It-to-'Em Sockarooni Spaghetti Sauce or your favorite

1 cup water

1 teaspoon sugar

1 teaspoon dried thyme leaves

1 teaspoon dried basil leaves

½ teaspoon salt

½ teaspoon coarsely ground black pepper

½ teaspoon dried oregano leaves

¼ teaspoon crushed red pepper flakes

1 bay leaf

In a 5-quart Dutch oven, sauté the onion in the butter over medium heat until tender and golden. Add the garlic and ham, and cook for 3 minutes. Add the remaining ingredients. Raise the heat to medium-high and bring to a boil, stirring. Remove the bay leaf before serving.

Franklin County, Florida's Own Frankly Fantastic Seafood Gumbo

Jackie Gay of Carrabelle, Florida, was the 1997 grand prize winner. She put on her lab coat for many an hour trying to achieve the perfect gumbo. Kudos to her for having created such a delectable combination of seafood and spices that any Cajun (or Yankee) would salute. She suggests serving saltine crackers on the side and says that other seafoods can be substituted. Her award went to the Friends of the Franklin County Public Library. Warning: This makes enough to serve thirty-two people!

■ SERVES 32

2 tablespoons vegetable oil

4 large purple and yellow onions, sliced

4 red, green, and yellow bell peppers, sliced

two 26-ounce jars Newman's Own All-Natural Diavolo Sauce or your favorite spicy sauce

1 tablespoon Cajun seasoning

1 teaspoon freshly ground black pepper

1 teaspoon cayenne pepper

1½ teaspoons salt

1 pint freshly shucked Apalachicola Bay oysters in their liquor

2 pounds shrimp, peeled and deveined

1 pound sea scallops

1 pound freshly cooked crab fingers, if available, or lump crabmeat

2 pounds grouper fillets or other firm fish fillets, such as scrod, cut into 1-inch pieces

1 pound fresh or frozen sliced okra

12 cups hot cooked high-quality white rice

Heat the oil in an 8-quart Dutch oven or saucepan over medium heat. Add the onions and the peppers and cook until slightly soft. Drain off the excess oil. Add the sauce, 3 cups of water, and all the seasonings. Turn the heat to low and simmer for 30 minutes. Add all the seafood and simmer for 45 minutes. Add the okra and simmer for 15 minutes. Serve immediately or refrigerate overnight.

To serve, reheat slowly, then put ½ cup of hot rice in each bowl and spoon 1 cup of the gumbo over it.

Towering Inferno Creole Posole

Alexandria Sanchez, who lives in Albuquerque, New Mexico, grew up on her Grandmother Sanchez's delicious posole. Now Alexandria has combined this traditional Mexican dish with the spicy flavors of Louisiana for a perfect blend of both cultures' cuisines. Along those lines, Alexandria suggests substituting 2 tablespoons "Cajun Spice" for the last four ingredients in the seasoning mix.

This was the 1997 grand prize recipe, and Alexandria donated her award to Tree New Mexico, Inc. ■ SERVES 10

SEASONING MIX

2 bay leaves

1½ teaspoons salt

1 teaspoon dried thyme leaves

2 teaspoons red chili powder or cayenne pepper

1 teaspoon white pepper

1 teaspoon freshly ground black pepper

1 teaspoon crushed red pepper flakes

VEGETABLE MIX

1 cup chopped celery (2 large stalks)

1 medium yellow onion, chopped

1 medium green bell pepper, chopped

3 tablespoons margarine or unsalted butter

8 ounces kielbasa (Polish sausage), cut into ½-inch pieces

12 ounces boneless, skinless chicken breast, cut into bite-sized chunks

1 tablespoon chopped garlic

2 cups Newman's Own Sock-It-To-'Em Sockarooni Spaghetti Sauce or your favorite

one to two 13¾- to 14½-ounce cans chicken broth

one 29-ounce can white hominy, drained (look for Mexican-style or *para posole*)

one 15-ounce can black beans, drained and rinsed

sour cream for garnish

grated Monterey Jack cheese for garnish

Combine the ingredients for the seasoning mix.

Combine the ingredients for the vegetable mix.

Melt the margarine in a heavy 5-quart Dutch oven (not nonstick) over medium heat. Add the kielbasa and sauté until the pieces begin to brown, about 3 minutes. Add the chicken and sauté for 5 minutes. Add the seasoning mix, vegetable mix, and garlic, and sauté until the vegetables start to soften, about 10 minutes. Add the sauce, 1 cup of the chicken broth, hominy, and black beans. Cover and simmer over low heat, stirring occasionally, for 20 minutes. Add more chicken broth if the mixture seems too thick.

To serve, remove the bay leaves. Spoon the posole into large bowls, top with a dollop of sour cream, and sprinkle with the cheese. Serve with warm thick flour tortillas (not the type for rolling) or rice.

Beef Stew with Potatoes and Pesto

This is a really fresh-tasting, fragrant stew, redolent not only of pesto but lots of fresh parsley. If tri-tip beef is not available in your market, use another good-quality cut, such as boneless sirloin. Standard stew meat just does not cut it here. As everyone knows (and if they don't, they should), mashed potatoes are the only possible accompaniment, along with a bottle of bold red vino. ■ MAKES 1 CUP OF PESTO SAUCE ■ SERVES 6

PESTO SAUCE

2 cups chopped basil leaves

3 cloves garlic, coarsely chopped

¼ cup fresh orange juice

¼ cup olive oil

¼ cup freshly grated Parmesan cheese

1 tablespoon pine nuts

salt and freshly ground black pepper to
    taste

4 small tomatoes

5 cloves garlic

2 tablespoons olive oil

4½ cups beef stock

¼ cup vegetable oil

1 medium-large red onion, diced

1½ pounds tri-tip beef, cut into 1-inch
    cubes

2 Idaho potatoes, peeled and cut into
    ½-inch dice

1 cup fresh or frozen white corn kernels

1 tablespoon Hungarian paprika

1 teaspoon ground coriander

1 bay leaf

salt and freshly ground black pepper to
    taste

1 cup chopped parsley

To make the pesto: Combine half of all the ingredients, not including the salt and pepper, in a blender and blend until smooth. Set aside in a bowl. Repeat with the remaining ingredients. Combine the 2 batches and season with salt and pepper.

Preheat the broiler.

Coat the tomatoes and garlic with olive oil and place on a baking sheet. Broil 4 inches from the heat, turning with tongs, until blackened all over, about 10 minutes. Transfer the vegetables with the tongs to a blender. Add enough stock to assist in blending until smooth.

Heat the vegetable oil in a pot over medium-high heat until hot. Add the onion and cook briefly, until soft. Add the beef and cook for 3 minutes, turning to brown evenly.

Add the potatoes, corn, paprika, coriander, and bay leaf. Cook 3 minutes more, stirring to combine. Add the tomato-garlic puree and the remaining stock, bring to a boil, then turn the heat to low. Cook, stirring occasionally to prevent scorching, for 50 minutes, or until the potatoes are tender but not falling apart. Season well with salt and pepper. Stir in the parsley and cook for 2 minutes. Turn off the heat, remove the bay leaf, and stir in ⅓ cup of the pesto.

Serve the stew in bowls garnished with a spoonful of the remaining pesto if desired.

Robert Redford's Lamb Chili with Black Beans

You can substitute beef or even chicken in this chili. Lamb does make it unusual and very good. It's the smoky flavor of the blackened tomatoes, though, that sends it over the top. ■ MAKES ABOUT 7 CUPS ■ SERVES 6

3 large tomatoes

½ cup vegetable oil

6 cloves garlic

½ medium red onion, diced

1½ pounds well-trimmed lamb stew
  meat, cut into 1- to 1½-inch cubes

2 tablespoons chili powder

1 tablespoon ground coriander

4 cups chicken stock

one 16-ounce can crushed tomatoes

1 tablespoon ketchup

1 tablespoon tomato paste

1 tablespoon Worcestershire sauce

1 cup canned black beans, drained

pinch of dried mint

salt and freshly ground black pepper to
  taste

GARNISH

3 tablespoons chopped onion

3 tablespoons chopped scallion

3 tablespoons sour cream

½ cup toasted pine nuts

Blacken the tomatoes in ¼ cup of oil in a very hot cast-iron skillet or under the broiler about 4 inches from the heat, turning them with tongs, until charred all over. (You can also char them without the oil; spear on the end of a long fork and hold over an open gas burner.)

Heat the remaining ¼ cup of oil in a large saucepan over high heat until hot. Add the garlic, onion, lamb, chili powder, and coriander, and cook, stirring, for 5 minutes. Add the blackened tomatoes, stock, crushed tomatoes, ketchup, tomato paste, and Worcestershire sauce. Turn the heat to medium and cook, stirring occasionally, for 35 minutes. Add the beans, mint, salt, and pepper. Turn the heat to medium-low and cook, stirring often to prevent scorching, for 10 minutes.

Serve the chili in large bowls garnished with ½ tablespoon each of onion, scallion, and sour cream per serving. Pass the nuts separately.

Vegetarian Black Bean Chili

Like most chilies and stews, this one gets better if left to stand overnight. To make a meal of this, you don't need much more than a good green salad, although a plate of Cornmeal Squares with Salsa (page 177) is a tasty addition. ■ MAKES ABOUT 7 CUPS ■ SERVES 6

¼ cup vegetable oil

1 medium red onion, chopped

8 cloves garlic

1 large carrot, diced

1 cup corn kernels

2 tablespoons ground cumin

1 tablespoon chili powder

1 bay leaf

¼ teaspoon crushed red pepper flakes (optional)

one 16-ounce can black beans, not drained

3 medium-large tomatoes, pureed

6 cups vegetable stock

2 drops liquid smoke (optional)

1 cup dark beer

salt and freshly ground black pepper to taste

GARNISH

6 teaspoons finely chopped red onion

6 teaspoons sour cream

6 tablespoons diced avocado

Heat the oil in a large pot over high heat until hot. Add the onion, garlic, carrot, corn, cumin, chili powder, bay leaf, and pepper flakes. Cook, stirring occasionally, for 5 minutes. Add the black beans, tomato puree, and vegetable stock, and bring to a boil. Turn the heat to medium-low and simmer for 15 minutes. Stir well, add the liquid smoke, and simmer 15 minutes more. Add the beer and cook another 20 minutes, stirring every now and then. Season well with salt and pepper.

Serve in bowls and garnish with a teaspoon each of the red onion and sour cream and a tablespoon of the avocado.

Main Courses

Butch's BBQ Sauce ▪ Matthew Broderick's Grilled T-bone Steak with Sweet Onion Marmalade and Campfire Mustard Sauce ▪ Danny Aiello's New York Strip Steak and His Cherokee Indian Curry AAA Steak Sauce ▪ Sundance's Salsa Steak in a Sack ▪ Whoopi Goldberg's Big Bad Ass Beef Ribs ▪ The Newmanburger ▪ Hud's Molasses-Grilled Pork with Port Wine Sauce ▪ Caroline Murphy's Ham Hocks and Beans ▪ Harry Belafonte's Pork, Apple, and Yam Salad with Honey Mustard Dressing ▪ Lamb Chops with Minty Marinade ▪ Lamb Shanks Inferno ▪ Brutus' Lamb Tagine Marrakech ▪ Tony Randall's

Grilled Veal Chop with Bourbon–Cracked Black Pepper Sauce ▪ Chicken with Orange Salsa Butter ▪ Grilled Chicken Paillards with Grilled Ratatouille and Romaine Hearts ▪ Lemon Mustard Chicken ▪ Caroline's Southern-Fried Chicken ▪ Martha Stewart's Chicken Cataplana ▪ Chicken Cassidy Kebabs and the Sundance Orzo Pilaf ▪ Greek Chicken Oregano Afloat in the Diavolo Drowning Pool ▪ Ismail Merchant's Yogurt Chicken ▪ Hotch Potch ▪ Hotch's Chicken Marinara ▪ Braised Chicken with "Say Cheese" Pasta Sauce, Mushrooms, and Walnuts ▪ Grilled Cumin Chicken Salad ▪ Cassidy's Chicken Curry ▪ Kiss of the Mediterranean Game Hens ▪ Incredible Cobb Salad ▪ Spice-Rubbed Roasted Turkey Breast ▪

The Grilled Bird of Youth Meets Judge Roy Bean

Salad ▪ Joanne Woodward's Sole Cabernet ▪

Joanne's Hollandaise Sauce ▪ Dilled Fillets of

Scrod à la Newman ▪ Italian Baked Scrod ▪

Mediterranean Fish Fillets ▪ Herbed Salmon Fillets in

Foil ▪ Salmon Supper Salad ▪ Hotchner's Spanish

Swordfish ▪ Walter Bridge's Grilled Swordfish

Steaks ▪ James Naughton's Honey Mustard Peppered

Tuna Steaks ▪ The Hustler's Grilled Tuna Steaks with

Caponata Relish ▪ Caroline Murphy's Tuna Salad ▪

Diavolo Seafood Loaves ▪ Garlic-Herb Marinated

Halibut with Lemon Sauce ▪ Sarah Jessica Parker's

Grilled Shrimp with Vodka-Lime Sauce ▪ Tasty Thai

Shrimp and Sesame Noodles ▪ Piquant Scallops with

Tangerines ▪ Joanne Woodward's Cioppino ▪ Blaze's

Shrimp and Sausage Creole ▪ Cool Hand Luke's

Brunch Burrito ▪ The Woodward Veggyburger ▪

Twice-Baked Potato over Spinach, Broccoli, and

Peppers ▪ Nell Newman's Marinated Ginger Tofu

over Crispy Browned Soba Noodles ▪ Potato and

Cheese Quesadillas with Green and Red Sauces ▪

Piñata Pockets

Pit Stop Pot Roast   Submitted by Sally Blitsch, Waterloo, Iowa

■ **SERVES 5**

3 pounds chuck pot roast	aluminum foil
1 cup Newman's Own Light Italian Salad Dressing	nonflammable cord
	200-mile trip

Twelve hours before the onset of the trip, place the roast in a glass bowl and cover the meat entirely with the dressing.

Place the roast on the aluminum foil. Wrap the roast in the foil and seal *tightly* on the top and at each end.

Fasten the wrapped meat securely on top of the manifold of the car or truck engine. Get into the car, fasten your seat belts, and begin your trip.

After 100 miles, turn the roast. Continue on the last 100 miles of the trip. At the end of the trip, the roast should be done and delicious.

If we ever have a plan, we're screwed!

—PAUL NEWMAN TO THE CHIEF
AUDITOR OF THE IRS

Butch's BBQ Sauce

There are many ingredients in this sauce, but once you make a batch of it, you'll have plenty on hand to use any time you like. It's a keeper in the refrigerator and freezes well, too. You might even consider splitting a batch and storing half in the refrigerator, half in the freezer.

This sauce figures prominently in a few four-star recipes in this chapter: Danny Aiello's New York Strip Steak and his Cherokee Indian Curry AAA Steak Sauce (page 65) and Whoopi Goldberg's Big Bad Ass Beef Ribs (page 68). A spoonful or two isn't bad on a well-constructed Newmanburger, either (page 69).

Don't confuse creamy horseradish sauce with the plain grated variety. You want a prepared creamy sauce here; it's usually sold in the condiment section of the supermarket. The granulated garlic is also found in many supermarkets. ■ MAKES 7 TO 8 CUPS

½ cup canola oil
½ cup chopped yellow onion
½ cup chopped garlic
4 cups tomato puree
1 cup packed dark brown sugar
1 cup Worcestershire sauce
¾ cup clover honey
¾ cup ketchup
½ cup creamy horseradish sauce
½ cup tomato paste

½ cup balsamic vinegar
½ cup Dijon mustard
¼ cup dark molasses
¼ cup dried onion
¼ cup granulated garlic
2 teaspoons salt
1 tablespoon freshly ground black pepper
1 bay leaf

Heat the oil in a large saucepan over medium-high heat until hot. Add the chopped onion and garlic, and cook, stirring, about 1 minute.

Add all the remaining ingredients and 2½ cups of water. Bring to a boil, stirring to dissolve the sugar. Simmer, stirring occasionally, for 20 minutes. Remove the bay leaf and let cool.

The sauce will keep in a covered container in the refrigerator for 2 months.

Matthew Broderick's Grilled T-bone Steak with Sweet Onion Marmalade and Campfire Mustard Sauce

Steak doesn't get any better than this, and when paired with Roasted Herbed New Potatoes with Spinach (page 166), it tastes too good to be true. If this seems like a lot of work, remember that both the marmalade and the campfire mustard sauce can be made up to four days in advance. Keep covered in the refrigerator. Then it's just a question of making the potatoes and grilling the steaks. It's well worth the effort.

■ SERVES 6

6 T-bone steaks (12 to 14 ounces each)
salt and freshly ground black pepper to
   taste

ONION MARMALADE

2 tablespoons unsalted butter
4 Vidalia onions, thinly sliced
6 shallots, thinly sliced
10 cloves garlic, thinly sliced
½ cup port wine
¼ cup balsamic vinegar

CAMPFIRE MUSTARD SAUCE

½ cup Dijon mustard
½ cup Pommery (French whole-grain)
   mustard
¼ cup honey mustard
¼ cup balsamic vinegar
1 teaspoon freshly ground black
   pepper

Bring the steaks to room temperature, then season with salt and pepper.

Meanwhile, make the onion marmalade: Melt the butter in a large cast-iron skillet. Add the onions, shallots, and garlic, and cook over high heat, stirring, for 10 minutes, until the onions are soft. Add the port and vinegar, and cook about 5 to 10 minutes, until the liquid is almost evaporated. Remove the pan from the heat but keep the marmalade warm.

To make the mustard sauce: Combine all the ingredients in a bowl.

Preheat a grill or broiler until hot. Grill the steaks for 4 to 4½ minutes per side for rare, 6 to 7 minutes per side for medium-rare.

Serve each steak topped with some warm marmalade. Serve the mustard sauce separately in a bowl.

Danny Aiello's New York Strip Steak and His Cherokee Indian Curry AAA Steak Sauce

It shouldn't take you more than about ten minutes to put this dynamite steak sauce together—which means you will have time to make Yam Gratin (page 170) and Caramelized East Indian Vegetables (page 162), both of which go stupendously well with these steaks. It also means you have a lot of really good eating in store.

You can find the red curry powder in Indian markets.

Leftover steak sauce will keep, covered and refrigerated, for about two weeks. Try it on chicken, too. ■ MAKES ABOUT 2¾ CUPS OF SAUCE ■ SERVES 6

CHEROKEE INDIAN CURRY AAA STEAK SAUCE

1 cup Butch's BBQ Sauce (see page 63) or your favorite brand
½ cup red wine vinegar
½ cup orange juice concentrate
¼ cup fresh lime juice
¼ cup vegetable oil
2½ tablespoons Madras curry powder
1 teaspoon red curry powder
1 teaspoon ground coriander powder
½ teaspoon salt
1 teaspoon freshly ground black pepper
¼ teaspoon ground allspice
1 tablespoon chopped garlic

6 New York strip steaks (8 to 10 ounces each, 1 inch thick)
salt and freshly ground black pepper to taste

To make the steak sauce: Combine all the ingredients in a large saucepan and add ½ cup of water. Cook over medium heat for 15 minutes. Let cool.

Place the steaks in a large shallow pan in 1 layer. Add 2 cups of the steak sauce and marinate for 30 minutes at room temperature. Turn and marinate 30 minutes more.

Grill, broil, or panfry the steaks to the desired doneness. Season with salt and pepper, and serve.

Sundance's Salsa Steak in a Sack

Julie DeMatteo, a 1992 finalist, was inspired by Paul Newman's movie *Butch Cassidy and the Sundance Kid* to create a recipe worth its weight in gold—golden bundles of phyllo pastry with tenderloin and salsa inside. Julie donated her award to Catholic Charities of Trenton and the Respiratory Distress Syndrome Foundation.

■ **SERVES 4**

4 beef tenderloin steaks (4 ounces each), 1 inch thick
½ teaspoon salt
½ teaspoon freshly ground black pepper
1 teaspoon olive oil
4 green onions or scallions
butter-flavored vegetable cooking spray

12 sheets phyllo pastry (17 x 12 inches), thawed
4 whole mild green chili peppers (from a 4-ounce can)
one 11-ounce jar Newman's Own All-Natural Bandito Salsa or your favorite

Butterfly the steaks. Sprinkle the cut surfaces with salt and pepper, and reclose the steaks. Panfry in the oil over medium-high heat for 1 minute per side, or until well browned. Remove to a plate.

Cut the white part off each onion and halve lengthwise. Cut the green of 1 onion top into 4 lengthwise strips.

Preheat the oven to 375°F. Lightly coat a baking sheet with the cooking spray.

Place 1 sheet of phyllo pastry on a clean, dry, flat surface. (Keep the remaining sheets from drying out by covering them with dampened paper towels.) Lightly coat the sheet with cooking spray, then fold in half lengthwise, sprayed side down. Place 1 steak in the center of the sheet. Insert 2 white pieces of a green onion, 1 chili pepper, and ¼ cup of salsa inside the steak. Fold the pastry over, forming a bundle, and coat with cooking spray. Place another sheet of phyllo on the work surface and coat with cooking spray. Top with a second sheet of phyllo and spray again. Place the steak bundle in the center of the stacked sheets and gather them around the bundle, gently pressing it together in the center so that the bundle resembles a sack tied in the middle. Tie a green strip of onion around the gathered part of the bundle.

Make 3 more bundles in the same way with the remaining ingredients.

Place the 4 bundles on the prepared baking sheet and spray the bundles and sheet again. Bake the bundles for 20 minutes, or until golden brown. (The meat will be well done.)

Serve with the remaining salsa.

You can get straight A's in marketing and still flunk ordinary life.

—PAUL NEWMAN TO LEE IACOCCA AFTER
IACOCCA'S PINTO CAUGHT FIRE

Whoopi Goldberg's Big Bad Ass Beef Ribs

Excellent with Potato Salad with Two Mustards Dressing (page 167). You'll have leftover marinade; use it in the same way you would any great steak marinade.

■ MAKES 3½ CUPS OF MARINADE ■ SERVES 6

18 beef ribs (not short ribs)

MARINADE

2 cups Butch's BBQ Sauce (page 63) or
    your favorite brand
½ cup Worcestershire sauce
⅓ cup fresh lemon juice
¼ cup Dijon mustard

2 tablespoons orange juice concentrate
2 tablespoons chopped garlic
1 tablespoon dark brown sugar
1 teaspoon powdered thyme
½ teaspoon salt
1 tablespoon freshly ground black
    pepper
1 teaspoon natural smoke flavoring

Place the ribs in a large pan of cold water and bring to a boil. Simmer, uncovered, for 45 minutes.

While the ribs are cooking, combine all the marinade ingredients in a large saucepan and bring to a boil. Simmer, stirring occasionally, for 15 minutes.

Preheat the oven to 325°F.

Drain the ribs and arrange in 1 layer in a large roasting pan. Pour 2 cups of marinade over them, brushing it on to cover both sides. Bake for 30 to 40 minutes, until the ribs are tender.

Serve with lots of napkins and a bowl of the remaining marinade on the side.

Newman and Whoopi at a camp gala

The Newmanburger

Don't make the mistake of using ground round or sirloin in this recipe; many hamburger cooks fall short of my standards because they use meat that is simply too good. I cook all my hamburgers on the outdoor grill or the indoor fireplace grill, and chuck is best suited to a hot charcoal fire.

ground chuck	tomatoes, sliced
vegetable oil	Bermuda onion, thinly sliced
hamburger buns	kosher dill pickles, slivered

Form the chuck into hamburger patties of the preferred size. I toss them from hand to hand to keep them fluffy. Never pat down the meat, or the hamburger won't be able to breathe while it's cooking. Also, never put salt, pepper, or any other seasoning in the meat before cooking because that will toughen it. The idea of adding onions, eggs, bread crumbs, or any other ingredient to the meat raises my hackles. Never confuse steak tartare with the pure hamburger.

Prepare the charcoal and grease the grill with vegetable oil, but don't put the meat on the fire until the charcoal is a uniform grayish white. Sear the burgers well on 1 side and turn them only once. After turning them, lower the grill for a brief time to sear the meat. The result: a hamburger that is crisp on the outside, tomato-red inside.

While the Newmanburgers are cooking, toast the buns around the edge of the grill. At my house, tomatoes, sliced onions, and pickles are the inevitable accompaniments. If corn is in season, it is also made part of the meal, always cooked for precisely 3 minutes and not a second longer in boiling, sweetened water. And a huge salad bowl, brimming with whatever fresh makings the market has to offer, is the table's centerpiece.

Although the Newmanburger is usually accompanied by frosty mugs of beer, on occasional impulse I serve up a bottle of Mouton-Rothschild or its equivalent, and that's when the Newmanburger tastes its best!

Hud's Molasses-Grilled Pork with Port Wine Sauce

Marie Terran, a 1996 runner-up, likes experimenting with food and made several attempts before finding the right balance of flavors to enhance but not overwhelm pork tenderloin. This recipe is sure to please Hud or that special someone. Marie donated her award to Aging Services for the Upper Cumberlands, Inc. ■ SERVES 6

¾ cup light molasses

¾ cup Newman's Own Olive Oil and Vinegar Dressing or your favorite

1½ to 1¾ pounds whole pork tenderloin

SAUCE

¾ cup port wine

½ cup dried cranberries or tart cherries or dark raisins

2 tablespoons Newman's Own Olive Oil and Vinegar Dressing or your favorite vinaigrette

1 tablespoon finely chopped shallot

1½ cups chicken broth

⅛ teaspoon cayenne pepper

1 tablespoon cracked black peppercorns

1 tablespoon cornstarch

2 tablespoons chicken broth

To prepare the pork: In a self-sealing plastic bag, mix the molasses and dressing. Add the pork tenderloin and seal the bag, pressing out as much air as possible. Marinate the pork in the refrigerator for at least 1 hour, turning occasionally.

To make the sauce: In a small bowl, mix together the port wine and cranberries. Set aside.

In a 2-quart saucepan, heat the 2 tablespoons dressing over medium heat, add the shallot, and cook for 2 to 3 minutes.

Drain the cranberries in a sieve set over a cup, pressing down on them to remove the port. Add the port to the hot dressing and bring the mixture to a boil over high heat. Boil for 1 minute, until reduced to ¼ cup. Add the 1½ cups of broth, cranberries, and cayenne pepper, and bring to a boil. Lower the heat to a simmer and cook the sauce until reduced by about half, 15 to 20 minutes.

While the sauce is simmering, preheat the grill.

Remove the pork from the marinade, reserving the marinade. Roll the pork in the cracked peppercorns, then place on the hot grill and sear over high heat. Lower the heat to medium and cook, turning and basting with the marinade every 5 minutes, for about 12 to 15 minutes, until the pork just loses its pink color. Remove and thinly slice.

Mix the cornstarch into the 2 tablespoons of broth. Stir the mixture into the reduced port sauce and bring to a boil. Remove the pan from the heat and serve the sauce over the pork.

It is useless to put on your brakes when you are upside down.

—PAUL NEWMAN TO A. E. HOTCHNER
AT THE SCENE OF THE CRASH

Caroline Murphy's Ham Hocks and Beans

My three favorite dishes all happen to be the culinary creations of my own household, which is, of course, gastronomically incestuous. Here's the recipe for my housekeeper's ham hocks and lima beans, which I would kill for.

■ SERVES 4

> 4 smoked ham hocks
> four 10-ounce packages frozen lima beans
> freshly ground black pepper

Cook the ham hocks in water to cover until almost tender. This will take 1 to 2 hours. Add the lima beans and pepper to taste. Cook until the beans are tender.

The only problem with this dish is that the ham hocks must be of top quality with lots of meat on them, and good ham hocks are hard to find. But if you tell your butcher in advance, he can usually turn up some good ones for you.

Harry Belafonte's Pork, Apple, and Yam Salad with Honey Mustard Dressing

Jalapeño Spoon Bread (page 175) was made for this salad. Time the two dishes so that you can serve the spoon bread warm—the only way to serve it. Start the spoon bread first, and while it is baking, put this warm salad together. It's easy to make and surprisingly light. Note that there is no oil in the dressing at all. If you can't get a pippin apple, substitute Cortland, Granny Smith, or Mutsu.

■ MAKES ABOUT ¾ CUP OF DRESSING ■ SERVES 6

DRESSING

½ cup honey mustard

2 tablespoons Worcestershire sauce

1 tablespoon balsamic vinegar

1 tablespoon freshly ground black pepper

1 teaspoon salt

SALAD

6 strips bacon, chopped, cooked, and drained, with drippings reserved

2¼ pounds pork tenderloin, diced

2 tablespoons olive oil

1 large yam, peeled and diced

1 pippin apple, unpeeled, cored, and diced

To make the dressing: Combine all the ingredients in a small bowl.

To make the salad: Put the bacon in a large serving bowl. Heat the drippings in a skillet until hot. Add the diced pork and cook, tossing, until barely medium-rare, about 3 minutes. Remove to a bowl.

Wipe the skillet clean, add the oil, and heat until hot. Add the yam and sauté until almost soft, about 5 minutes. Add the apple and cook, tossing, for 1 minute. Add to the serving bowl with the bacon.

Return the pork to the skillet and finish cooking it, tossing, about 7 minutes. Immediately add the pork to the serving bowl, pour in the dressing, and toss.

Serve at once while the pork is still warm.

Lamb Chops with Minty Marinade

Suggesting a cooking time for meat is a tricky issue. One person's medium is another's well done. With a cut as extravagant as double-thick lamb chops, err on the side of undercooking them. You can always cook them a little more. The best way to judge when meat is properly cooked is by hand, something all good chefs do instinctively. When you think the meat you're cooking is done, press down on the thickest part with your finger. The meat will bounce back slowly for rare. The longer the meat cooks, the faster it will regain its shape. For well done there will be no indentation at all.

Make Garlicky Mashed Potatoes (page 164) to go with these chops.

■ MAKES ABOUT 1½ CUPS OF MARINADE ■ SERVES 6

MARINADE

¾ cup mint Worcestershire sauce

½ cup olive oil

¼ cup balsamic vinegar

¼ cup fresh orange juice

juice of 2 lemons

2 tablespoons chopped yellow onion

1 tablespoon finely chopped mint leaves

1 teaspoon chopped garlic

1 teaspoon ground cumin

1 teaspoon powered ginger

1 teaspoon salt

1 tablespoon freshly ground black pepper

12 double-thick rib lamb chops, 6 to 7 ounces each

salt and freshly ground black pepper

olive oil for searing the chops

To make the marinade: Mix all the ingredients together well in a large glass bowl or jar. The marinade will keep, covered and refrigerated, for 2 weeks.

Season the chops with salt and pepper, then put them in a single layer in a large shallow pan. Pour in 1 cup of the marinade and let stand for 1 hour at room temperature.

To grill or roast the chops: Preheat the grill or oven to 400°F. If roasting, heat 2 tablespoons of the oil in each of 2 cast-iron skillets until hot. Add the chops and sear on both sides until golden. Transfer the skillets to the oven and roast for 5 minutes per side for rare, 7 to 8 minutes per side for medium-rare. If grilling, cook the chops for 9 minutes per side or to the desired degree of doneness.

Serve 2 chops per person, with about 2 tablespoons of marinade spooned over the meat.

Lamb Shanks Inferno

Sue Bloom of Rhinebeck, New York, won the 1994 grand prize with this spicy dish. Sue donated her award to the Tufts University School of Veterinary Medicine.

Serve with mashed potatoes, egg noodles, or rice. ■ SERVES 4

4 lamb shanks
salt and freshly ground black pepper to taste
¼ cup flour
6 tablespoons olive oil
1 small onion, diced
2 cloves garlic, minced
1 carrot, diced
¾ cup dry red wine
¾ cup beef broth
one 26-ounce jar Newman's Own All-Natural Diavolo Sauce or your favorite spicy sauce
parsley sprigs for garnish

Preheat the oven to 350°F.

Season the lamb shanks with salt and pepper, and dredge them in the flour; tap off the excess. Heat 5 tablespoons of the oil in a 5-quart Dutch oven until medium-hot. Add 2 of the lamb shanks, brown them all over, then set aside. Repeat with the remaining 2 lamb shanks.

Scrape the brown bits off the bottom of the pan and discard. Heat the remaining 1 tablespoon of oil in the Dutch oven until medium-hot. Add the onion and garlic, and sauté until soft and translucent. Add the carrot and sauté for 1 to 2 minutes. Add the red wine, raise the heat to high, and reduce the wine by half. Add the beef broth and sauce, and bring just to a boil. Immediately remove the pan from the heat.

Add the lamb shanks to the Dutch oven, spoon the sauce over them, and cover tightly. Bake for 2 hours, or until the meat is fork-tender.

Remove the shanks and keep them warm. Skim the fat from the sauce. Adjust the seasonings.

Serve the lamb shanks with the sauce and garnish with the parsley sprigs.

Brutus' Lamb Tagine Marrakech
Newman's Own Caesar Dressing serves as the perfect marinade for lamb shoulder. It is then presented in a flavorful sauce featuring prunes marinated in sherry, mixed with a mélange of spices, and Newman's Own All-Natural Bandito Salsa. "Tagine" is the Moroccan word for stew; hence, Marrakech.

Barbara Morgan, 1995 runner-up, donated her award to the Enchanted Hills Summer Camp for the Blind. ■ MAKES ABOUT 1 CUP OF SAUCE ■ SERVES 12

one 12-ounce package pitted prunes
⅔ cup dry sherry
3 pounds lean lamb shoulder, cut into 1½-inch cubes
one 8-ounce bottle Newman's Own Caesar Dressing or your favorite
2 large onions, finely chopped
3 cloves garlic, finely chopped
1 small knob of gingerroot, peeled and shredded
1 to 2 teaspoons finely chopped jalapeño pepper
two 13¾- to 14½-ounce cans chicken broth

3 carrots, peeled and sliced
2 baking potatoes, peeled and diced
½ cup Newman's Own All-Natural Bandito Salsa (Medium) or your favorite
2 tablespoons fresh lemon juice
1 tablespoon chopped fresh thyme
1 tablespoon ground cumin
1 teaspoon ground turmeric
1 teaspoon Hungarian paprika
¼ cup chopped cilantro

Preheat the oven to 375°F. Cover the prunes with the sherry and soak for 15 minutes or longer.

Place the lamb cubes and dressing in an airtight container or zippered plastic bag and coat the cubes thoroughly. Marinate in the closed container for at least 1 hour in the refrigerator.

Remove the lamb from the marinade with tongs and discard the marinade. In a 12-inch skillet, brown the lamb in batches over medium-high heat, then transfer to a 5-quart Dutch oven.

In the same skillet, sauté the onions over medium heat for 10 minutes. Add the garlic and sauté 3 minutes more. When the onions are translucent, mix in the gingerroot and jalapeño and cook for 2 minutes. Transfer the mixture to the Dutch oven.

Add the broth, carrots, potatoes, salsa, lemon juice, thyme, cumin, turmeric, and paprika, and bring to a boil. Add the prunes with the sherry. Cover and bake for 45 minutes, or until the lamb and vegetables are tender. Stir in the cilantro.

Serve over egg noodles.

Just when things look darkest they go black.

—PAUL NEWMAN TO
WALTER MONDALE, 1984

Tony Randall's Grilled Veal Chop with Bourbon–Cracked Black Pepper Sauce

A peppery bourbon butter sauce enhances the subtle flavor of veal here. Serve with Braised Root Vegetables (page 169); they look good on the plate, taste great, and come in handy when you're hunting down the last of this blue-ribbon sauce. ■ SERVES 6

6 rib veal chops (10 to 12 ounces each)
salt and freshly ground black pepper to
    taste
2 tablespoons olive oil

BOURBON SAUCE

¼ cup dry red wine
¼ cup dry white wine

½ cup bourbon
1 stick (8 tablespoons) cold unsalted
    butter, cut into tablespoons
salt to taste
1½ teaspoons coarsely cracked fresh
    black pepper

Preheat your grill until hot or preheat the oven to 350°F.

Season the veal chops well with salt and pepper.

If you are grilling the chops, rub them with the oil. Place on the grill, leaving room between. Grill for 7 to 10 minutes per side, turning once. If the chops are 1½ inches thick, cook 9 to 12 minutes per side.

If you are roasting the chops, heat the oil in a large cast-iron skillet over high heat until hot. Add the chops and sear on 1 side only. Transfer the skillet to the oven and roast the chops for 10 to 12 minutes more for medium-rare.

While the chops are cooking, make the sauce. In an enamel or other nonreactive saucepan, combine the red and white wines and cook over high heat until hot. Add the bourbon and cook until reduced by half.

Lower the heat to medium and add the butter, 1 piece at a time, quickly whisking it in until completely incorporated. You want to blend each piece of butter in fully, not just melt it, before adding the next. Work quickly but do not increase the heat under the sauce. Season with salt and cracked black pepper, and keep warm in a warm water bath until ready to use. Do not reheat the sauce over direct heat.

Place a grilled chop on each dinner plate and spoon about 2 tablespoons of the bourbon sauce over the top. Serve immediately.

Tony in the camp's skewed version of Cinderella

Chicken with Orange Salsa Butter

Salsa and a little orange zest perk up the mild flavor of white meat chicken. This is quick and good, and as mild or spicy as the salsa you use. Serve over pilaf or spinach pasta. ■ SERVES 4

4 tablespoons unsalted butter at room temperature

4 tablespoons Newman's Own All-Natural Bandito Salsa or your favorite

1 teaspoon grated orange zest

½ cup flour

½ teaspoon salt

¼ teaspoon cayenne pepper

2 whole chicken breasts (8 ounces each), skinned, boned, and halved

¼ cup fresh orange juice

2 tablespoons vegetable oil

orange slices for garnish

In a food processor, process the butter, salsa, and orange zest until smooth. Spoon the butter onto a sheet of plastic wrap and shape into a log. Wrap tightly and freeze.

Combine the flour, salt, and cayenne on a plate.

Dip the chicken pieces, 1 at a time, in the orange juice and then in the seasoned flour; shake off the excess. Discard the juice.

Heat the oil in a large nonstick skillet over medium-high heat. Add the chicken in 1 layer and cook, turning once, until golden brown and cooked through, about 7 to 8 minutes depending on thickness. Place on dinner plates.

Cut the cold orange butter into 4 pieces and put a piece on each chicken breast. Garnish with orange slices and serve at once.

Dear Sirs:

A miracle happened while eating a salad with your delicious dressing. Some dropped on my shoe. I ran and got a paper towel and rubbed it off—haven't seen a shine on my shoes like that for 81 years. Now I use it every day for shining my shoes and putting on my salad. Even tried it on furniture, and it worked. So you have a product to double your money. Your sales would go up 10 percent if you let people know your dressing is good for shoes and furniture polish.

With your knowledge of products, I am sure you could make a cake out of it for shoe shining.

J.F.

Grilled Chicken Paillards with Grilled Ratatouille and Romaine Hearts

Arnauld Briand, former executive chef of the Rainbow Room complex atop Rockefeller Center in New York City, created this elegant yet lean entree. ■ SERVES 4

4 whole, skinless, boneless chicken
    breasts
freshly ground black pepper
one and a half 8-ounce bottles
    Newman's Own Light Italian
    Dressing or your favorite dressing
2 tablespoons minced garlic
2 sweet onions (Walla Walla or
    Vidalia), cut into thick slices

1 zucchini, cut into ¼-inch slices
1 yellow squash, cut into ¼-inch slices
1 medium eggplant, cut into ½-inch-
    thick slices
2 heads romaine lettuce
cherry tomatoes
fresh herbs

Pound the chicken breasts into paillards, about ¼ inch thick. Sprinkle with pepper and marinate in ½ cup of dressing and 1 tablespoon of garlic for 2 hours.

Marinate the onions, zucchini, squash, and eggplant in ½ cup of the remaining dressing and the remaining 1 tablespoon of garlic.

Preheat the grill.

Grill the chicken breasts and vegetables over hot coals until charred but not burned and the chicken is cooked through, about 3 minutes per side.

Arrange the grilled vegetables on 4 plates, leaving the center empty. Remove the outside leaves of the lettuce and chop the hearts. Place the chopped lettuce in the center of each plate. Place the grilled chicken on the lettuce and spoon some of the remaining ½ cup of dressing over the top. Garnish with the cherry tomatoes and fresh herbs.

Lemon Mustard Chicken

Mustard and chicken go together, and lemon and chicken do, too, so it follows that mustard, lemon, and chicken would make an excellent combination. It does. If you don't have walnut oil, substitute 1½ teaspoons of dark sesame oil. ■ SERVES 4

2 whole, large, skinless, boneless
   chicken breasts, halved
1 cup Newman's Own Old-Fashioned
   Roadside Virgin Lemonade or your
   favorite
¼ cup fresh bread crumbs
¼ cup finely chopped pecans or
   walnuts

1 egg
5 tablespoons whole-grain mustard
vegetable oil for frying
3 to 4 teaspoons walnut oil
½ cup chicken broth
¼ cup heavy cream
salt and freshly ground black pepper to
   taste

Marinate the chicken in the lemonade for 1 hour. Drain, reserving the lemonade, and pat the chicken dry with paper towels.

Stir together the bread crumbs and nuts on a plate. Put the egg in a shallow bowl and beat lightly. Place 3 tablespoons of the mustard in another bowl.

Brush the chicken with the mustard, dip into the beaten egg, then dredge in the crumbs and nuts. Chill, loosely covered, for 2 to 3 hours.

Heat ½ inch of the vegetable oil with the walnut oil in a large skillet until hot. Add the breaded chicken and fry, turning once, for 10 to 12 minutes. Remove to a plate and keep warm.

While the chicken is cooking, combine the reserved lemonade, broth, and the remaining 2 tablespoons of the mustard in a small saucepan. Bring to a boil and reduce over high heat to ½ cup. Add the cream and cook about 1½ minutes to heat through and thicken slightly. Season with salt and pepper, and pour over the chicken. Serve hot.

Caroline's Southern-Fried Chicken Our housekeeper, Caroline Murphy, has taken several of the dishes she sets on our table and contributed them to this book. Her Ham Hocks and Beans (page 72) is one of my all-time favorites, her Tuna Salad is unmatched (page 115), and her southern-fried chicken is out of this world. ■ SERVES 2 TO 3

1 fryer (about 3 pounds), cut up	Herbamare or Spike (see seasoning
sea salt	Note)
paprika	2 cups vegetable oil

Season the chicken well with the sea salt, paprika, and Herbamare. Refrigerate for 1 hour to let the seasonings penetrate the chicken.

Heat the oil to very hot and fry the chicken for 12 to 15 minutes per side. Keep the lid on to prevent splattering and help the chicken cook faster.

NOTE: Spike seasoning is a mixture of assorted herbs and seaweed. It can be found in most health food stores.

Martha Stewart's Chicken Cataplana

A cataplana is a copper Portuguese cooking pan. If you don't have one, use a small Dutch oven with a tight-fitting lid instead. This is a great one-dish meal, essentially a meat-and-potatoes combination, but it's light. ■ SERVES 4

2 tablespoons olive oil

1½ cups Newman's Own All-Natural Bandito Salsa or your favorite

2 medium potatoes, peeled and thinly sliced

2 whole, skinless, boneless chicken breasts, halved

1 medium onion, thinly sliced

1 teaspoon dried oregano

salt and freshly ground black pepper to taste

Preheat the oven to 350°F.

Place the oil in the bottom of the cataplana or Dutch oven. Add half of the salsa. Top with a layer of sliced potatoes, chicken breasts, and onions. Top with the remaining salsa and sprinkle the oregano over it. Season with salt and pepper. Cover and bake for 1½ hours.

Chicken Cassidy Kebabs and the Sundance Orzo Pilaf

Aban Lal paired spiced chicken kebabs with a savory pilaf studded with colorful fruits, vegetables, and almonds, and enriched with cheese, to become a finalist in 1994. He donated his award to Habitat for Humanity and UNICEF. ■ SERVES 6

2 pounds skinless, boneless chicken breasts, cut into 2-inch cubes or pieces

MARINADE

1 cup Newman's Own Olive Oil and Vinegar Dressing or your favorite

2 teaspoons fresh gingerroot, ground into a paste

2 teaspoons garlic paste

¾ teaspoon or less cayenne pepper

SUNDANCE ORZO PILAF

3 cups freshly cooked orzo

1 cup Newman's Own Olive Oil and Vinegar Dressing or your favorite

⅓ cup orange juice concentrate

½ cup minced mint

2 tablespoons or less red chili oil

1 teaspoon minced gingerroot

½ cup chopped dried apricots

1 cup currants

1 cup toasted slivered almonds

1 cup sun-dried tomatoes packed in oil, chopped

1 large green bell pepper, diced

1 cup minced red onion

1 cup cubed goat cheese (optional)

thin orange slices for garnish

mint sprigs for garnish

Place the chicken in a glass dish or nonreactive bowl.

Mix the marinade ingredients together and pour over the chicken. Cover and refrigerate for at least 5 hours or overnight, turning occasionally.

Remove the chicken from the marinade and thread on 12 soaked wooden skewers.

To make the pilaf: Place the orzo in a large bowl. In another bowl, whisk together the dressing, orange juice concentrate, mint, chili oil, and gingerroot. Pour the dressing over the orzo and mix well. Add the remaining ingredients and toss gently. Cover the bowl and keep at room temperature while the kebabs cook.

Preheat the grill. When ready to serve, grill or broil the skewers for about 5 to 6 minutes per side.

Transfer the orzo to a serving tray. Arrange the cooked chicken skewers attractively on top. Garnish with the orange slices and mint sprigs.

> Whenever I do something good, right away I've got to do something bad, so I know I'm not going to pieces.
>
> —PAUL NEWMAN, 1985

Greek Chicken Oregano Afloat in the Diavolo Drowning Pool

Developing a recipe using Newman's Own All-Natural Diavolo Sauce was easy for Helen Conwell. She found that the spicy base melds perfectly with and enhances the flavors found in traditional Mediterranean cuisine. Helen, a 1995 finalist, donated her award to Ecumenical Ministries of the Eastern Shore Literacy Council. ■ SERVES 8

4 whole chicken breasts, halved
salt
1 large onion, sliced
1 clove garlic, minced
2 tablespoons olive oil
one 26-ounce jar Newman's Own All-Natural Diavolo Sauce or your favorite
1 bay leaf
2 tablespoons minced fresh oregano
1 tablespoon minced fresh thyme
1 teaspoon ground cinnamon
one 10-ounce package frozen artichoke hearts, cooked according to package directions
1 tablespoon fresh lemon juice
½ teaspoon sugar
salt to taste
one 8-ounce package orzo, cooked according to package directions
1 tablespoon minced parsley
oregano sprigs for garnish

Preheat the broiler. Sprinkle the chicken with the ½ teaspoon of salt. Broil the chicken, skin side up, 5 to 7 inches from the heat until blistered and browned, about 10 minutes. Set aside.

Meanwhile, in a deep 12-inch skillet, sauté the onion and garlic in 1 tablespoon of the oil over medium heat until softened, about 10 to 12 minutes. Add the sauce, bay leaf, oregano, thyme, and cinnamon. Scrape up any brown bits from the bottom of the skillet.

Add the chicken, cover, and simmer for 30 minutes, turning once after 15 minutes, until the juices run clear. Add the artichoke hearts, lemon juice, and sugar. Remove the chicken, place in a bowl, and keep warm.

Boil the sauce, uncovered, until it thickens and the artichoke hearts are heated through. Add salt to taste.

Toss the orzo with the parsley and the remaining 1 tablespoon of oil. Arrange the orzo on 2 sides of a serving platter. Arrange the chicken mixture in the middle and spoon the sauce over it. Garnish with the oregano sprigs.

Ismail Merchant's Yogurt Chicken
(Dahi Murgh) ■ SERVES 10 TO 12

½ cup vegetable oil

2 medium onions, chopped

4 dried whole red chiles

12 cloves

5½ pounds chicken drumsticks and thighs

1-inch piece of fresh gingerroot, peeled and grated

1½ cups plain yogurt

1 teaspoon salt

1 tablespoon freshly ground black pepper

Heat the oil in a large heavy-bottomed frying pan or saucepan over medium heat. When hot, add the onions, chiles, and cloves. Cook, stirring frequently, until the onions brown.

Add the chicken and gingerroot, and stir continually until the meat is seared on all sides.

Mix the yogurt with 1 cup of water. Add to the pan with the salt and pepper. Cover and cook over medium-low heat, stirring occasionally, for 1 hour.

Hotch Potch
You can actually throw anything that's handy into the pan, and it will fit right in with this dish. ■ SERVES 4

4 medium potatoes, peeled, quartered, and parboiled

3 tablespoons cooking oil

1½ pounds chicken breasts, skinned, boned, and cut into bite-sized pieces

3 tablespoons butter or margarine

1 medium onion, coarsely chopped

1 stalk celery, coarsely chopped

1 green bell pepper, seeded and coarsely chopped

1 red bell pepper, seeded and coarsely chopped

2 medium tomatoes, peeled and chopped

pepper

Worcestershire sauce to taste

¼ cup soy sauce

In a heavy pan, brown the potatoes well in half of the oil. Remove and set aside. Brown the chicken pieces in the same pan, lower the heat, and continue cooking, stirring occasionally. While the chicken is cooking, prepare the vegetables.

In a separate pan set over medium-high heat, sauté the onion and celery in the butter until golden. Add the peppers and toss for about 1 minute. Add the tomatoes, pepper, Worcestershire sauce, and soy sauce. Simmer for 1 to 2 minutes, add the chicken and potatoes, stir together, and serve.

Hotch's Chicken Marinara
The Italian-style stuffing of spinach and cheese is a savory surprise in this easy-to-prepare dish.

■ **SERVES 4**

2 large skinless, boneless chicken breasts, halved

4 tablespoons unsalted butter or oil

1 small onion, diced

1 pound fresh spinach or one 10-ounce package frozen chopped spinach

¼ cup ricotta cheese

2 tablespoons freshly grated Parmesan cheese

⅛ teaspoon ground nutmeg

one 26-ounce jar Newman's Own All-Natural Spaghetti Sauce with Mushrooms or your favorite

8 ounces spinach noodles or linguine

Preheat the oven to 350°F.

Form a pocket in the underside of each chicken breast, where the bone was removed, for the stuffing.

Heat 2 tablespoons of the butter. Add the onion and sauté until golden.

Wash and stem the spinach if fresh and cook in the water that clings to the leaves, about 2 minutes. Drain well and chop. If using frozen spinach, thaw and drain well. Combine with the onion in the pan. Remove from the heat and add the cheeses and nutmeg.

Stuff a few tablespoons of the mixture in each chicken breast. Fold the ends of the chicken under to enclose the filling. Spread the remaining butter on the bottom of a baking dish. Arrange the chicken pieces in the dish, stuffed side down. Pour the sauce over the chicken and bake for 45 to 50 minutes.

Cook the noodles and serve with the chicken breasts, spooning sauce over all.

Braised Chicken with "Say Cheese" Pasta Sauce, Mushrooms, and Walnuts

As executive chef and director of Manhattan's Rainbow Room complex, Waldy Malouf has the formidable challenge of overseeing pretheater, dinner, and late-night supper in the Rainbow Room, dinner and supper in the Rainbow and Stars cabaret, as well as the bar and Sunday brunch menus in the Promenade Bar.

Malouf also represents Rainbow's commitment to charity as a participating chef for Share Our Strength's Taste of the Nation. In addition, he represents Rainbow's commitment to hunger-relief causes and culinary education by volunteering his services at many events, including God's Love We Deliver, The Culinary Institute of America, Citymeals-on-Wheels, the James Beard House, and Farmhands-Cityhands. ■ SERVES 4

8 pieces of chicken: such as breasts, thighs, or legs
coarse salt and freshly ground black pepper
flour for dredging
¼ cup vegetable oil
8 ounces quartered mushrooms

½ cup dry white wine (optional)
one 26-ounce jar Newman's Own "Say Cheese" Pasta Sauce or your favorite

GARNISH

½ cup chopped walnuts
¼ cup chopped fresh parsley or basil

Preheat the oven to 375°F.

Pat the chicken dry with paper towels, season with salt and pepper, and dredge in flour, shaking off the excess.

Heat the oil in a 12-inch ovenproof skillet. Add the chicken pieces, skin side down, and brown over medium heat for 7 to 8 minutes, until crisp and golden. Turn the chicken over and cook 3 to 4 minutes more. Remove the chicken from the pan and set aside. Continue to cook the fat until the solids stick to the pan without burning and the fat is clear. Discard the fat, add the mushrooms, and cook for 3 minutes. Add the wine and bring to a simmer, stirring to incorporate the browned bits. Reduce by half. Add the sauce and bring to a boil. Return the chicken to the pan, skin side up.

Place the pan in the oven and bake the chicken, uncovered, for 10 minutes. Remove the breast pieces and keep warm. Cook the dark meat 5 minutes more. Transfer the chicken to a serving casserole and pour the sauce over it. Sprinkle the walnuts and parsley on top.

You want to get a bead on a new restaurant? Order something you don't like. If you like it, you got a bead on a new restaurant.

—PAUL NEWMAN

Grilled Cumin Chicken Salad

If you make the dressing and bake the tortillas in advance, this is an easy salad to put together and great for hot weather get-togethers. You can also broil the chicken if it's too cold or inconvenient to use the grill. Try it with Joanne Woodward's Gazpacho (page 47).

■ **MAKES ABOUT 1½ CUPS OF CUMIN DRESSING** ■ **SERVES 6**

CUMIN DRESSING

¼ cup Dijon mustard

¼ cup distilled white vinegar

¼ cup fresh lemon juice

4 tablespoons ground cumin

1 tablespoon finely chopped shallot

¾ cup canola oil

½ teaspoon salt

1 tablespoon finely ground black pepper

3 tablespoons ground cumin

3 tablespoons canola oil

3 whole, skinless, boneless chicken
   breasts

salt and freshly ground black pepper to
   taste

2 corn tortillas

olive oil

SALAD

2 medium heads romaine lettuce,
   chopped

2 Roma tomatoes, diced

1 cup thinly sliced scallion, green and
   white parts

1 ripe avocado, diced

½ medium hothouse cucumber, diced

½ small red onion, cut into julienne
   strips

½ cup chopped and pitted Niçoise
   olives

To make the cumin dressing: In a bowl, stir together the mustard, vinegar, lemon juice, cumin, and shallots. Add the oil slowly, whisking it in until combined. Season with salt and pepper. Transfer the dressing to a covered container and refrigerate until ready to use.

In a shallow, flat dish, combine the cumin and oil. Add the chicken and turn to coat with the mixture. Season to taste with salt and pepper. Refrigerate while you prepare the tortillas and salad.

Preheat the oven to 375°F. Cut the tortillas into julienne strips and place on a baking sheet. Sprinkle the pieces very lightly with olive oil, salt, and pepper. Bake, turning them, until golden brown, 5 to 10 minutes.

Combine the salad ingredients in a large serving bowl.

Preheat the grill until hot.

Grill the chicken breasts, turning them, about 12 minutes per side, until no longer pink inside. Transfer to a plate, let cool, then shred the chicken. Add to the salad.

Just before serving, add the tortillas to the salad with ¾ cup of the dressing and toss. Serve with the remaining dressing on the side if desired.

Cassidy's Chicken Curry

Gloria Bradley of Naperville, Illinois, took Newman's Own on an exotic and flavorful trip through Southeast Asia, and discovered that the mild buttermilk flavor of Newman's Own Ranch Salad Dressing serves to accentuate the characteristic Asian flavors of coconut milk, curry powder, coconut, peanuts, and fresh basil. Gloria, a 1995 finalist, donated her award to the Misericordia Home for Children. ■ SERVES 4

1 tablespoon olive oil
1 medium onion, chopped
2 cloves garlic, minced
1 large red bell pepper, cut into thin
    strips
1 large green bell pepper, cut into thin
    strips
2 whole, skinless, boneless chicken
    breasts (about 1¼ pounds), cut into
    ¾-inch pieces
2 tablespoons fresh lime juice

1 tablespoon curry powder
8 tablespoons coconut milk (not cream
    of coconut)
½ cup Newman's Own Ranch Dressing
    or your favorite
2 tablespoons chopped fresh basil or
    2 teaspoons dried
½ teaspoon crushed red pepper flakes
3 cups hot cooked rice
peanuts, chopped cilantro, and
    shredded coconut as toppings

Heat the oil in a 12-inch nonstick skillet over medium-high heat until hot. Add the onion and garlic, and cook for 2 minutes. Add the peppers and cook, stirring, until lightly browned. Remove the mixture to a small bowl.

Add the chicken pieces to the skillet with the lime juice, curry powder, and 2 tablespoons of the coconut milk. Cook until the chicken loses its pink color throughout, about 4 to 5 minutes.

Stir in the remaining 6 tablespoons of coconut milk, the dressing, basil, and red pepper flakes. Add the pepper mixture and cook over medium heat about 5 minutes, until heated through.

Serve the curry over the hot cooked rice with the toppings on the side.

Kiss of the Mediterranean Game Hens

Lotte Mendelsohn, who hosts "Dining Around with Lotte Mendelsohn" on WRKO radio in Boston and is food editor of TAB newspapers there, was the 1995 food pro finalist. She donated her award to the Boys and Girls Club of the Monterey Peninsula. Lotte recommends serving this over seasoned rice. ■ SERVES 4

2 large Cornish game hens (1½ to 2 pounds each), halved

salt and freshly ground black pepper to taste

3 tablespoons virgin olive oil

2 cloves garlic, halved

1 rounded teaspoon ground cinnamon

¼ teaspoon ground cloves

3 tablespoons balsamic vinegar

½ cup blanched almonds

2 tablespoons fresh basil leaves

one 14-ounce jar Newman's Own Bombolina Spaghetti Sauce or your favorite

lemon zest curls for garnish

Preheat the oven to 425°F.

Rinse and pat the hens dry with paper towels. Lightly salt and pepper the insides.

Heat the oil in a shallow flameproof baking pan. Lightly brown the garlic, but do not let it burn. Remove and discard the garlic. Add the hens to the garlic oil and brown on both sides. Pour off the excess oil and fat in the pan and arrange the hens skin side down.

Make a paste of the cinnamon, cloves, and 2 tablespoons of the vinegar. Brush half of it on the exposed undersides of the hens. Bake for 10 minutes more. Turn the hens and brush with the remaining spice paste. Bake for 10 minutes more.

Meanwhile, in a mini-mixer or blender, coarsely grind the almonds. Add the basil leaves and process until the mixture has the consistency of coarse sand. In a bowl, blend the remaining 1 tablespoon of vinegar with the almond mixture and sauce.

Pour the sauce over the hens, brushing some of it on the undersides. Bake, skin side up, for 10 to 15 minutes, or until the almond paste bubbles slightly.

Serve garnished with the lemon zest curls.

Incredible Cobb Salad

Incredible Cobb Salad This variation of the classic lunch salad includes most of the expected ingredients in the traditional recipe, plus some dandy surprises. Toss well with a judicious amount of dressing and have extra on the side. You can also serve this in hollowed-out whole-grain rolls.

The yolks of the six hard-boiled eggs don't make an appearance in this updated version. If you want, do include them.

■ MAKES ABOUT 2 CUPS OF DRESSING ■ SERVES 6

DRESSING

½ cup crumbled French blue cheese

2 tablespoons Dijon mustard

1 teaspoon very finely minced garlic

⅓ cup fresh lemon juice

1 teaspoon Worcestershire sauce

⅓ cup distilled white vinegar

1 cup vegetable oil

½ teaspoon salt

1 teaspoon freshly ground black pepper

2 tablespoons olive oil

1 small zucchini, diced

1 small red bell pepper, diced

1 small yellow bell pepper, diced

1 Japanese eggplant, diced

salt and freshly ground black pepper to taste

3 skinless, boneless chicken breast halves, cooked and cut into cubes

6 slices turkey bacon, cooked and diced

6 hard-boiled eggs, peeled, yolks removed, and the whites chopped

1 small head Napa cabbage, shredded

2 avocados, diced

¼ cup crumbled French blue cheese

To make the dressing: In a food processor, combine ¼ cup of the blue cheese, the mustard, garlic, lemon juice, Worcestershire sauce, and vinegar, and blend. The mixture will be thick. Add the oil in a thin, steady stream and ⅓ cup of water. Blend until smooth. Add the salt and pepper, and blend 10 seconds more. Pour the dressing into a bowl and stir in the remaining ¼ cup of blue cheese. Cover and let stand for 1 hour at room temperature before serving.

Heat the oil in a large skillet over high heat until hot. Add the zucchini, peppers, and eggplant, and sauté, tossing. Add ¼ cup of water and cook a total of 6 minutes, until crisp-tender. Season lightly with salt and pepper. Drain off any remaining liquid and let cool in a large mixing bowl.

Add the chicken, bacon, chopped egg whites, cabbage, avocados, and blue cheese to the sautéed vegetables and toss well. Pour on the dressing to taste and toss again. Serve the remaining dressing in a bowl on the side.

There are three rules for running a business. Fortunately, we don't know any of them.

—A. E. HOTCHNER TO PAUL NEWMAN
AS THEY SENT 804,000 CONTAINERS
OF LEMONADE TO THE TROOPS IN
DESERT STORM

Spice-Rubbed Roasted Turkey Breast

This herb-and-spice-coated turkey breast goes very well with Creamy Potato Salad (page 168). If you're thinking of making a picnic of this—and this makes good picnic food—double the salad. The granulated garlic is available at most supermarkets.

■ **SERVES 8 TO 10**

1 boneless turkey breast (4 to 4½ pounds)

buttermilk for soaking the turkey breast

SPICE RUB

¼ cup cumin seeds

¼ cup dried rosemary

¼ cup granulated garlic

¼ cup dried parsley flakes

1 teaspoon salt

1 tablespoon freshly ground black pepper

1 tablespoon olive oil

The day before you plan to cook the turkey breast, put it in a bowl, cover it with buttermilk, cover the bowl, and place in the refrigerator overnight.

The next day, preheat the oven to 450°F.

In a small bowl, toss all the spice rub ingredients together.

Remove the turkey breast from the buttermilk, letting the milk drip off. Pat the spice rub evenly all over the turkey breast, pressing it on. Place in a small baking pan and cover the pan with aluminum foil.

Bake for 35 minutes. Lower the temperature to 375°F, uncover the turkey breast, and bake 25 minutes more, until nicely browned.

Remove the turkey breast from the oven and place on a cutting board. Let cool, then cut into thin slices.

The Grilled Bird of Youth Meets Judge Roy Bean Salad

Doyle Haeussler was motivated at an early age to be highly creative with fowl: While growing up, there was an overabundance of it in her parents' freezer! Newman's Own Olive Oil and Vinegar Salad Dressing is the secret ingredient in her recipe of grilled duck breast served over a salad of cannellini beans. Doyle, a 1995 grand prize winner, donated her award to the Special Olympics of Indiana, the U.S. Holocaust Memorial Museum, and the Community Association of Muncie and Delaware Counties. ■ SERVES 4

2 boneless duck breasts, halved (or
    2 whole, skinless, boneless chicken
    breasts, halved)
1 cup Newman's Own Olive Oil and
    Vinegar Dressing or your favorite
8 ounces mixed salad greens
two 19-ounce cans cannellini beans,
    rinsed and drained
½ cup chopped green onions

½ cup loosely packed, finely chopped
    flat-leaf parsley
¼ cup packed, finely chopped basil
    leaves
1 pint red and/or yellow pear-shaped
    or cherry tomatoes, each cut in half
1 red bell pepper, cut into thin strips
1 yellow bell pepper, cut into thin strips

Place the duck in a bowl with ½ cup of the dressing. Cover and refrigerate overnight.

Preheat the grill.

Drain the duck, discarding the marinade, and pat dry with paper towels. Grill the duck over medium heat, preferably over aromatic wood or charcoal, until no longer pink inside when cut and the skin is crisp and browned. Or broil the duck in a preheated broiler for 7 to 8 minutes. (If using chicken, grill until the meat is no longer pink inside when cut, about 4 minutes per side.)

Divide the salad greens among 4 dinner plates. Toss the cannellini beans with the remaining ½ cup of dressing, the onions, parsley, and basil. Top the greens with the bean mixture. Arrange some tomato halves and pepper strips around the plate.

Slice the duck breasts on the diagonal and lay the slices over the top of the salads. Serve with additional dressing if desired.

Joanne Woodward's Sole Cabernet This is at the top of my list of favorite dishes. It is in a class by itself. ■ SERVES 4

4 tablespoons unsalted butter

4 fillets of sole (2 to 2½ pounds)

salt and freshly ground black pepper to
  taste

2 shallots, chopped

2 cups good cabernet sauvignon

1 cup Joanne's Hollandaise Sauce
  (recipe follows)

Preheat the oven to 375°F.

Put dabs of butter on the fillets of sole and fold them over crosswise. Add the salt, pepper, and shallots. Place in a baking pan and add the cabernet sauvignon. Bake for 10 minutes, then remove the fish to a plate.

Pour the wine sauce into a saucepan and reduce to ⅓ the original amount. Let cool. Add Joanne's Hollandaise Sauce to the wine sauce. Return the sole and sauce to the baking pan. Place in the oven for 5 minutes before serving.

Joanne's Hollandaise Sauce ■ MAKES 2 CUPS

3 egg yolks

3 tablespoons cold water

1 stick (8 tablespoons) lightly salted
  butter, melted

freshly ground pepper to taste

juice of ½ lemon

Place the egg yolks and water in the top of a double boiler over hot but not boiling water. Whisk rapidly until the mixture thickens and an instant-read thermometer registers 160°F. Remove from the heat. Add the butter, little by little, while continuing to whisk. Add the pepper. Add the lemon juice just before serving.

Dilled Fillets of Scrod à la Newman

Coming in a distant second to Joanne's Sole Cabernet is my own dilled fillet of scrod, which I bake in the oven, liberally coating it with lots of fresh dill, butter, and lemon juice. ■ SERVES 4

2 pounds scrod fillets

3 to 4 tablespoons chopped fresh dill or 1 tablespoon dried

1 stick (8 tablespoons) unsalted butter

¾ cup dry white wine

1 cup Joanne's Hollandaise Sauce (page 103)

Preheat the oven to 375°F.

Wash the fillets and pat dry with paper towels. Arrange in a single layer in a 13 x 9 x 2-inch baking dish. Cover with the dill. Heat the butter and wine together in a small saucepan until the butter melts. Pour over the fish. Bake for 20 minutes, or just until the fish separates easily when touched with a fork.

Serve with Joanne's Hollandaise Sauce.

Italian Baked Scrod

This is really a variation on Dilled Fillets of Scrod (page 104), but the resulting flavor is so different that it deserves a page of its own. The amount of onions, tomatoes, and olives is entirely up to you.

■ SERVES 4

2 pounds scrod fillets
salt and freshly ground black pepper to
    taste
sliced onions
chopped stewed tomatoes
sliced pitted ripe olives

2 tablespoons chopped fresh basil or
    1 tablespoon dried
2 tablespoons chopped fresh parsley or
    1 tablespoon dried
1 clove garlic, crushed
clam juice

Preheat the oven to 375°F.

Wash the fillets and pat dry with paper towels. Arrange in a single layer in a 13 x 9 x 2-inch baking dish. Season with salt and pepper. Cover with the onions, tomatoes, olives, basil, parsley, and garlic. Moisten with a little clam juice.

Bake for 20 minutes, or just until the fish separates easily when touched with a fork. Drain off most of the liquid before serving.

Mediterranean Fish Fillets

Up the ante here by stirring a little pesto into basmati rice to serve with these easy-to-make, quick-cooking fillets. The black olive paste is available in jars at the supermarket. ■ SERVES 4

2 tablespoons black olive paste

1 tablespoon Dijon mustard

4 red snapper or flounder fillets (about 2 pounds)

½ cup Newman's Own Bombolina Spaghetti Sauce or your favorite

4 sun-dried tomatoes packed in oil, cut into thin strips

2 teaspoons fresh lemon juice

½ teaspoon grated lemon zest

¼ cup toasted slivered almonds

shredded fresh basil leaves for garnish

grated lemon zest for garnish

Combine the olive paste and mustard in a small bowl.

Preheat the oven to 500°F. Coat a baking sheet with oil.

Fold the ends of each fillet under to form a square, then spread some of the olive paste mixture on top. Arrange the squares on the prepared baking sheet and bake for 12 to 15 minutes, or until the fish separates easily when touched with a fork.

Meanwhile, in a small saucepan, heat the sauce with the tomatoes, lemon juice, and zest over medium heat until hot.

When the fillets are done, transfer to plates and spoon some of the hot sauce on top. Garnish with the almonds, basil, and lemon zest. Serve at once.

Herbed Salmon Fillets in Foil

These packets make entertaining very easy because they can be prepared entirely in advance—first thing in the morning, if you like—and kept in the refrigerator until cooking time. Just as important, they take only twelve minutes to cook. Serve with Balsamic Eggplant and Potatoes (page 163) for a dynamite combination. ■ SERVES 6

6 salmon fillets (6 ounces each)

salt and freshly ground black pepper to taste

6 thin lemon slices

1 cup Newman's Own Caesar Dressing or your favorite

¼ cup chopped garlic

1 tablespoon chopped fresh thyme

3 cups whole wheat croutons

Preheat the oven to 450°F. Have ready 6 pieces of aluminum foil, each cut to enclose 1 fillet.

Place a fillet in the middle of a piece of foil. Season with salt and pepper, and put a lemon slice on top. Pour 2½ tablespoons of dressing over each fillet. Sprinkle with the garlic and thyme, and scatter ½ cup of croutons over each fillet. Enclose in the foil, sealing it airtight and leaving a little space at the top for the packet to expand.

Bake the packages on the rack of the oven for 12 minutes. (The packets will puff up slightly.) Transfer the packages to dinner plates. Be sure to open them carefully because there is a buildup of steam inside.

Salmon Supper Salad

You can serve these salads for either lunch or supper, along with soup to round out the meal, or as a very appealing, substantial first course of a simplified dinner menu. You will have leftover dressing. It's good on almost any kind of salad.

■ **MAKES 1 GENEROUS CUP OF DRESSING** ■ **SERVES 6**

DRESSING

¼ cup balsamic vinegar

¼ cup fresh lime juice

2 tablespoons Dijon mustard

¼ cup chopped chives

1 shallot, chopped

1 teaspoon ground cumin

½ cup olive oil

salt and freshly ground black pepper to taste

1 pound mixed baby greens

2 tomatoes, chopped

1 bunch scallions, thinly sliced

½ small red onion, thinly sliced

1½ avocados, diced

3 salmon fillets (6 to 7 ounces each)

olive oil for brushing the salmon

salt and freshly ground black pepper to taste

To make the dressing: Combine the vinegar, lime juice, mustard, chives, shallot, and cumin in a blender or food processor and blend until combined. With the motor running, add the oil in a slow, steady stream, blending until emulsified. Season with salt and pepper. Transfer the dressing to a container and let stand for 1 hour at room temperature before serving.

Preheat the grill.

In a large bowl, combine the greens, tomatoes, scallions, red onion, and avocados.

Brush the salmon fillets with the oil on both sides and arrange in a hinged grill pan. Grill for 6 to 8 minutes on each side, depending on the thickness. (You can also cook the fillets in a preheated grill pan on the top of the stove for the same amount of time per side.) Let the salmon fillets cool, then remove the skin. Crumble the salmon into bite-sized chunks and add to the salad with ⅓ cup of the dressing. Toss gently and add salt and pepper. Serve with additional dressing on the side if desired.

Dear Mr. Newman:

I wish to commend and compliment you on the excellence and versatility of your salad dressing, Newman's Own Oil and Vinegar Dressing. . . . The other day I took a walk on the beach during my lunch hour, which is how I normally spend my lunches. This was preceded by a light but satisfying meal of a green salad topped by Newman's Own Olive Oil and Vinegar Salad Dressing. As I was saying, I took a walk on the beach, in the fine City of Solana Beach, and the only proper way to walk on the beach is to go barefoot. . . .

When I got back to work, still barefoot, I noticed a large patch of tar which I had apparently stepped in while walking. . . . Well, Mr. Newman (may I call you Paul?), I remembered my lunch and your fine-tasting oil and vinegar dressing—and you know what, it really did the trick! Two applications of Newman's Own to the bottom of my foot really cut through the grease and grime and took that tar patch right off, baby. Not only is your product a treat for the palate, but it's also a great cleaning agent—and biodegradable, too—truly a product for all seasons. . . .

MOST SINCERELY,
K.J.

Hotchner's Spanish Swordfish

Hemingway and I used to eat at a little restaurant on the beach at Torremolinas in southernmost Spain, run by an old Basque fisherman. We were so smitten by this swordfish that I asked the old man to show me how to cook it. I once tried to cook it on a grill in Ketchum, Idaho, but the swordfish was frozen and had no taste. Now I often show it off in Connecticut when the local fish store alerts me to a swordfish fresh off the hook.

Make sure the pine bough you use has not been sprayed with pesticides. Rinse and dry it well before using. ■ SERVES 4 TO 6

2 pounds swordfish steak, 2 inches thick and cut evenly
1 cup Newman's Own Salad Dressing, Newman's Vinaigrette Dressing (page 30), or your favorite
¼ cup fresh lime juice

3 tablespoons fresh thyme or rosemary, or 1 tablespoon dried plus additional for cooking
lemon juice
butter
1 small freshly cut pine bough

Marinate the swordfish in the salad dressing, lime juice, and thyme or rosemary for several hours in the refrigerator.

Prepare a charcoal grill and place the fish on the grill when the coals are gray. Saturate with lemon juice, chunks of butter, and more thyme. Cook for 10 minutes on each side, turning only once. Baste with more lemon juice and marinade, and dot with butter after turning. Remove the fish, place the pine bough on the fire, put the fish on top, and let it be seared by the flame. Remove after the pine flame dies down and serve immediately.

Walter Bridge's Grilled Swordfish Steaks

Paul Newman's starring role as Walter Bridge (who loved to spark up the grill!) inspired Cynthia Mitchell to develop this hassle-free swordfish recipe. Fresh from the fisherman's net, the swordfish is marinated and basted with a wine-laced sauce of Newman's Own Ranch Dressing, fresh herbs, citrus juices, and capers. The secret lies in the simplicity of preparation. Cynthia, a 1996 runner-up, donated her award to Friends of Homeless Animals. ■ SERVES 4

one 8-ounce bottle Newman's Own Ranch Dressing or your favorite
¼ cup dry white wine
2 tablespoons fresh lemon juice
2 tablespoons fresh lime juice
1 tablespoon chopped fresh rosemary
1 tablespoon chopped fresh dill
1 tablespoon minced capers
2 swordfish steaks (12 ounces each), 1 inch thick
lemon and lime slices for garnish
rosemary sprigs for garnish

In a 13 x 9-inch baking dish, stir the dressing, white wine, lemon juice, lime juice, rosemary, dill, and capers together until blended. Cut the swordfish steaks crosswise in half and add to the marinade, turning to coat them. Cover and refrigerate at least 1 hour, turning occasionally.

Preheat the broiler.

Remove the swordfish steaks, reserving the marinade, and place on a rack in a broiling pan. Broil as close to the heat source as possible for 8 to 10 minutes without turning, until the fish flakes easily when tested with a fork. Brush once halfway through the broiling time with some of the reserved marinade. Discard the remaining marinade.

(You can also grill the swordfish. About 45 minutes in advance of serving, preheat the grill. Grill the swordfish over medium heat for approximately 5 minutes per side. Brush once halfway through the grilling with the reserved marinade. The fish is done when it flakes easily when tested with a fork. Discard the remaining marinade.)

Place the swordfish on a platter and garnish with the lemon and lime slices and rosemary sprigs.

James Naughton's Honey Mustard Peppered Tuna Steaks

This seared fresh tuna on a bed of lightly seasoned cucumber and tomato salad is cooked until barely warm. It is meant to be very rare inside, so if you don't like rare tuna, this dish is not for you. You can substitute halibut, scrod, or cod, however, and cook them until opaque throughout.

If you're a tuna lover, you will need the freshest, best-quality tuna you can lay your hands on. First choice is ahi ahi, which is also the most expensive and may not always be available. Second would be yellowfin. Securing the tuna, we'd wager, will be the most time-consuming part of making this stylish entree. You could also serve this in smaller portions as a first course at a dinner party.

■ MAKES 1 CUP OF DRESSING ■ SERVES 6

SALAD

2½ cups chopped tomatoes

2½ cups matchstick slices hothouse cucumber

2 tablespoons olive oil

2 tablespoons seasoned rice vinegar

salt and freshly ground black pepper to taste

DRESSING

½ cup tamari sauce

¼ cup seasoned rice vinegar

2 tablespoons Chinese hot mustard

2 tablespoons fresh lemon juice

1 tablespoon finely chopped basil

1 tablespoon finely chopped shallots

1 teaspoon minced ginger

TUNA

¾ cup honey mustard

salt to taste

2 tablespoons coarsely ground black pepper

6 tuna steaks (6 to 7 ounces each), cut 1 inch thick, or halibut, scrod, or cod steaks

toasted sesame seeds for garnish (optional)

To make the salad: Toss together all the ingredients in a bowl. Let stand at room temperature for 1 hour before serving.

To make the dressing: In another bowl, whisk all the ingredients together well.

Preheat the broiler.

To prepare the fish: In a small bowl, combine the mustard, salt, and pepper. Place the fish on a cookie sheet and generously brush on one side only with the mustard mixture. Place on the lowest rack and broil for 4 to 6 minutes with no turning. (If using halibut, scrod, or cod, broil for 5 to 8 minutes with no turning.)

To serve, divide the salad among 6 plates and top with the fish. Spoon 3 tablespoons of dressing over the fish and serve the remaining dressing on the side. Garnish with the toasted sesame seeds.

James Naughton and Julia Roberts cavorting at the 1997 camp gala

The Hustler's Grilled Tuna Steaks with Caponata Relish

Rachel Sancilio of Virginia Beach, Virginia, loves to cook for her children and grandchildren. Her caponata, which can be made ahead of time, is a sure bet and a crowd pleaser. Rachel, a 1996 runner-up, donated her award to the Children's Hospital of the King's Daughters at Johns Hopkins Hospital. ■ SERVES 8

3 celery sticks, cut into ½-inch pieces

2 medium onions, cut into ½-inch pieces

3 tablespoons olive oil

salt

1½ pounds eggplant, cut into ½-inch pieces

1 cup Newman's Own Bombolina Spaghetti Sauce or your favorite

½ cup white wine vinegar

½ cup sliced pitted ripe olives

½ cup sliced pitted green olives

¼ cup sugar

2 tablespoons capers, drained

½ teaspoon dried basil leaves

¼ teaspoon crushed red pepper flakes

freshly ground black pepper

8 tuna steaks (about 6 ounces each), 1 inch thick

1 ounce pine nuts, toasted, for garnish

Preheat the oven to 425°F.

In a 13 x 9-inch roasting pan, toss the celery and onions together with 1 tablespoon of the oil and ¼ teaspoon of salt. In a 17 x 11½-inch roasting pan, toss the eggplant with the remaining 2 tablespoons of oil and ¼ teaspoon of salt. Put the pans in the oven on 2 different racks and roast the vegetables for 20 minutes, tossing them once halfway through the roasting time.

Combine all the roasted vegetables in a larger roasting pan. Add the sauce, vinegar, olives, sugar, capers, basil, red pepper flakes, and ¼ teaspoon of black pepper. Toss to mix well. Cover the pan with foil and bake in the oven for 30 minutes. Remove and keep warm.

Turn the oven to broil. Place the tuna steaks on a rack in a broiling pan and sprinkle lightly on both sides with salt and black pepper. Broil as close to the heat source as possible for 4 to 5 minutes for rare, 10 minutes for well done, or until opaque throughout.

Serve the caponata, garnished with pine nuts, alongside the tuna steaks.

Caroline Murphy's Tuna Salad
This is another one of my favorites and just one of our housekeeper's triumphs. I like it as a sandwich on Nell's Sesame Loaves (page 180). ■ SERVES 2 TO 3

one 6½-ounce can tuna	3 tablespoons mayonnaise
1 teaspoon mustard	3 scallions, finely chopped
1 whole sweet pickle, minced	1 tablespoon sweet pickle juice

Drain the tuna and flake into a bowl. Add the remaining ingredients and mix well. Serve as a salad or sandwich filling.

Diavolo Seafood Loaves

Christine Loughridge showcases two of the finest products of the Pacific Northwest—sourdough bread and seafood—in her 1991 winning recipe. She donated her award to the Crohn's and Colitis Foundation of America. ■ SERVES 4

1 to 1½ pounds fresh seafood (red snapper, shrimp, or whatever is available)

4 loaves sourdough bread, each about 5 inches long

olive oil or a mixture of butter and oil

3 cloves garlic, chopped

2 scallions, chopped

1 cup dry white wine

1 small red bell pepper, diced

1 small yellow bell pepper, diced

1 small green bell pepper, diced

one 26-ounce jar Newman's Own All-Natural Diavolo Sauce or your favorite

1 bunch cilantro (to make 1 cup chopped and 8 whole sprigs for garnish)

softened butter

tomato slices and orange slices for garnish

Preheat the oven to 400°F.

Clean or shell the seafood. Slice the top off each loaf, then hollow out the loaf to within 1 inch of the sides. Cut the removed bread into cubes and put in a bowl. Drizzle with a little oil and ⅓ of the garlic, and toss. Bake the croutons on a baking sheet, tossing once, for 10 minutes, or until golden brown.

Heat 3 tablespoons of oil in a skillet. Add another ⅓ of the garlic and the scallions, and sauté over medium heat until the scallions are softened. Add the wine and reduce to ½ cup. Add the seafood and peppers, and sauté, stirring, just until the seafood is no longer transparent. Do not overcook. Remove the pan from the heat.

In a saucepan, heat the sauce and stir in the chopped cilantro.

Turn on the broiler.

Spread the softened butter on the inside of each hollowed-out loaf and sprinkle with the remaining garlic. Put the loaves under the broiler to brown lightly.

To assemble, put ¼ of the seafood mixture into each loaf and add ¼ of the sauce, filling to within 1 inch of the top. Sprinkle with the croutons, garnish with the cilantro sprigs, and lean the top of the loaf alongside. Fill and finish the remaining loaves in the same way.

To serve, arrange the seafood loaves on a platter and garnish with the tomato and orange slices.

Garlic-Herb Marinated Halibut with Lemon

Sauce If you want to go all out, serve the halibut on a bed of Garlicky Mashed Potatoes (page 164), with a sauté of snow peas, carrots, and red onion on the side. The lemon sauce is good on almost anything. When it comes to seasoning the fish, though, only fresh herbs as a crust will do.

■ **MAKES ABOUT ½ CUP OF SAUCE** ■ **SERVES 6**

6 Alaskan halibut steaks (about 7
    ounces each)
1½ cups chopped mixed fresh herbs,
    such as basil, parsley, cilantro, and
    tarragon
1 tablespoon minced garlic
¼ cup olive oil

LEMON SAUCE
7 tablespoons unsalted butter, cut into
    tablespoons
1 tablespoon chopped garlic
½ cup dry white wine
¼ cup fresh lemon juice
1 tablespoon soy sauce
salt and freshly ground black pepper to
    taste

In a shallow baking dish large enough to hold the halibut in 1 layer, combine the herbs, garlic, and oil. Add the halibut steaks and turn to coat them on both sides with the herb mixture. Cover and refrigerate for 1 hour before cooking.

Preheat the broiler.

While the broiler is heating, make the lemon sauce: In an enamel saucepan, melt 1 tablespoon of the butter over medium heat. Add the garlic and cook, stirring, until golden. Stir in the wine, lemon juice, and soy sauce, and reduce the liquid by ⅓. Add the remaining 6 tablespoons of butter, 1 piece at a time, quickly whisking until completely incorporated. You want to fully blend each piece, not just melt it, before adding the next. Taste and add salt and pepper. Keep the sauce warm in a warm water bath until ready to use. Do not reheat the sauce over direct heat.

Broil the halibut on a broiling pan on the middle rack of the oven for about 6 to 8 minutes, or until just cooked through and the juices run clear when tested with a fork. (You can also roast the halibut in a preheated 475°F oven for 8 to 10 minutes with no turning.)

Serve the halibut with several tablespoons of the lemon sauce drizzled over the top.

Sarah Jessica Parker's Grilled Shrimp with Vodka-Lime Sauce

Very good as is, but if you serve these shrimp with Honey Mustard Mashed Potatoes (page 165), they are even better. Arrange the shrimp, tails up, in a mound of the potatoes, then drizzle on the butter sauce. There is something really fine in the way the mustard in the potatoes and the lime in the sauce intermingle. ■ MAKES ABOUT ¾ CUP OF SAUCE ■ SERVES 6

36 extra-large shrimp, peeled and
    deveined but with tails on
2 tablespoons olive oil
salt and freshly ground black pepper to
    taste

VODKA-LIME SAUCE

1 cup vodka
1 cup dry white wine

⅓ cup fresh lime juice
1½ sticks (12 tablespoons) cold
    unsalted butter, cut into
    tablespoons
salt and freshly ground black pepper to
    taste

¾ cup sliced scallion, green and white
    parts, for garnish

In a shallow flat-bottomed dish, combine the shrimp with the oil, salt, and pepper. Let stand at room temperature while preheating the grill.

Preheat the grill.

To make the vodka-lime sauce: In an enamel or glass saucepan, combine the vodka, wine, and lime juice. Reduce the mixture over medium heat to ⅓ the original amount. Add the butter, 1 piece at a time, quickly whisking in until completely incorporated. You want to blend each piece of butter in fully, not just melt it, before adding the next. Work quickly but do not increase the heat under the pan. Season with salt and pepper. Keep the sauce warm in a warm water bath until ready to use. Do not reheat the sauce over direct heat.

Arrange the shrimp in 1 layer in a hinged grill pan. Grill over a hot fire for 4 minutes per side, or until just cooked through. You can also sauté them in batches, using 1 tablespoon of olive oil per batch, in a hot cast-iron skillet for 4 minutes per side.

To serve, put 5 shrimp on each plate, spoon 2 to 3 tablespoons of sauce over them, and sprinkle scallion rings on top. Serve at once.

Tasty Thai Shrimp and Sesame Noodles

Exotic flavorings reminiscent of Far East cuisine blend together with Newman's Own Light Italian Dressing in a light, fast, and easy Asian dish created by Beverly Ann Crummey of Brooksville, Florida. Now this restaurant favorite and 1993 grand prize winner can be enjoyed at home, week in and week out. Beverly Ann donated her award to Daystar Life Center. ■ SERVES 4

1 pound medium shrimp, peeled and deveined

one 8-ounce bottle Newman's Own Light Italian Dressing or your favorite

2 tablespoons chunky peanut butter

1 tablespoon soy sauce

1 tablespoon honey

1 teaspoon grated peeled gingerroot

½ teaspoon crushed red pepper flakes

8 ounces cappellini or angel hair pasta

2 tablespoons salad oil

1 tablespoon sesame oil

1 medium carrot, peeled and shredded

1 cup chopped green onions

¼ cup chopped cilantro for garnish

In a medium bowl, mix the shrimp with ⅓ cup of the dressing, cover, and refrigerate for 1 hour.

In a small bowl, whisk together the peanut butter, soy sauce, honey, gingerroot, red pepper flakes, and the remaining dressing.

When the shrimp has finished marinating, drain and discard the dressing. Bring a large pot of salted water to a boil, add the pasta, and cook according to the package directions until firm but tender.

Meanwhile, in a 4-quart saucepan, heat the salad oil and sesame oil over high heat until very hot. Add the carrot and cook for 1 minute. Add the drained shrimp and green onions, and cook, stirring constantly, for about 3 minutes, or until the shrimp are opaque throughout.

Drain the pasta, place in a large bowl, and add the peanut sauce and shrimp mixture. Toss to combine. Garnish with the chopped cilantro and serve.

Piquant Scallops with Tangerines

The sea scallops "cook" here first in vinegar, then in a lemony, gingery marinade. Try this for lunch on a hot summer day, when light eating is in order. Or halve the portions and serve it as an appetizer. Serve with chilled crisp white wine as an accompaniment. ■ SERVES 4

12 ounces sea scallops, cut into quarters if large
¾ cup cider vinegar
⅓ cup Newman's Own Old-Fashioned Roadside Virgin Lemonade or your favorite
1 tablespoon honey
1½ teaspoons walnut oil
2 tablespoons finely diced green bell pepper
½ clove garlic, finely minced

1½ teaspoons finely minced peeled gingerroot
pinch of cayenne pepper
salt and freshly ground black pepper to taste
1 head radicchio, finely shredded
whole cilantro sprigs to taste
2 or 3 tangerines, peeled and membranes removed
1 tablespoon chopped chives (optional)

In a ceramic or glass bowl, marinate the scallops in the vinegar, covered, in the refrigerator for 1 hour. Drain and discard the vinegar. Rinse the scallops under cold running water and drain well.

In another glass bowl, combine the scallops with the lemonade, honey, oil, green pepper, garlic, gingerroot, cayenne pepper, salt, and pepper. Toss, cover, and marinate in the refrigerator, stirring occasionally, for 1½ hours.

Make a bed of shredded radicchio on each of 4 plates and add whole cilantro sprigs. Divide the scallops among the plates and arrange tangerine sections around the sides. Drizzle with the marinade and sprinkle with chives. Serve chilled.

Joanne Woodward's Cioppino

Serve with crusty Italian bread. To round out the meal, add a salad of romaine lettuce with slivers of cheese and walnuts, tossed with your favorite vinaigrette. ■ SERVES 6

¼ cup salad or olive oil

2 cloves garlic, minced

2 medium onions, chopped

2 green bell peppers, seeded and chopped

one 26-ounce jar Newman's Own All-Natural Marinara Style Venetian Spaghetti Sauce or your favorite

1 cup dry white wine

1½ pounds cod, sliced and cut into pieces

8 ounces frozen lobster tails, shelled and cut up

1 pound mussels and/or small clams

Heat the oil in a deep, heavy skillet or Dutch oven. Add the garlic, onions, and peppers, and cook until the onions are golden. Add the marinara sauce, wine, cod, and lobster, and simmer for 6 minutes. Add the mussels, cover, and cook 5 minutes more, until the fish is done and the shellfish are open.

Blaze's Shrimp and Sausage Creole

Sergeant Mark Maki finds cooking and experimenting with different cuisines great stress therapy. Inspired by Cajun cooking, Mark created a quick and easy Creole recipe—a hassle-free dinner for any day of the week. He donated the money from his 1995 grand prize to Covenant Christian School. ■ SERVES 6

2 tablespoons unsalted butter or margarine

2 celery stalks, chopped

1 medium yellow bell pepper, chopped

1 large yellow onion, chopped

12 ounces kielbasa, sliced

1 clove garlic, minced

1½ cups clam juice

1 cup Newman's Own Bombolina Spaghetti Sauce or your favorite

SPICE MIXTURE

1 bay leaf

½ teaspoon dried thyme leaves

½ teaspoon dried basil leaves

½ teaspoon salt

½ teaspoon white pepper

¼ teaspoon cayenne pepper

¼ teaspoon freshly ground black pepper

1 pound medium shrimp, peeled and deveined

3 cups hot cooked rice, prepared according to package directions

In a 12-inch skillet, heat the butter or margarine over medium-high heat until hot. Add the celery and pepper, and sauté for 8 to 10 minutes, until softened. Remove the mixture from the skillet and set aside. Add the onion and kielbasa to the skillet and sauté for 10 minutes. Stir in the garlic and cook for 30 seconds.

Add the clam juice, sauce, and all the spice mixture ingredients, and bring to a boil. Cover and simmer for 5 minutes. Add the shrimp and cook for 2 to 3 minutes, until the shrimp turn opaque throughout. Add the reserved celery mixture and heat through. Remove the bay leaf.

To serve, spoon the hot rice into large shallow soup bowls and top with the shrimp and sausage Creole.

Cool Hand Luke's Brunch Burrito

Paul Newman's movie provided the inspiration for Timothy Conrad's recipe, which naturally contains scrambled eggs. Timothy said, "Cool Hand Luke's hard-boiled bet may have been easier to swallow if he had followed my recipe." Timothy gave his award from this 1991 contest winner to the Columbus Children's Hospital.

■ SERVES 4

2 tablespoons salad oil
8 ounces bulk sausage
2 jalapeño peppers, seeded and chopped
1 medium onion, chopped
2 cups Newman's Own All-Natural Diavolo Sauce or your favorite
8 eggs
salt and freshly ground black pepper to taste
1 tablespoon unsalted butter
4 large flour tortillas, warmed
4 ounces Monterey Jack cheese, shredded
4 cups shredded lettuce
1 lime, sliced

In a large nonstick skillet, heat 1 tablespoon of the oil over medium heat. Add the sausage and cook thoroughly, until no pink shows. Remove from the skillet and drain on paper towels. Wipe the fat from the pan.

In the same skillet, heat the remaining 1 tablespoon of oil over medium heat. Add the jalapeño peppers and onion, and cook, stirring, until tender. Add the sauce and sausage, and cook for 5 minutes.

In a bowl, beat the eggs with ¼ cup of water, salt, and pepper. In another skillet, melt the butter over medium heat, pour in the eggs, and cook, stirring, for 4 minutes. Stir in half of the sausage and sauce mixture.

Preheat the broiler.

Spoon ¼ of the egg mixture onto each tortilla, then roll up the tortillas and place in an ovenproof or microwave-safe serving dish. Pour the remaining sausage and sauce over the tortillas and sprinkle the cheese on top. Broil or microwave the tortillas until the cheese melts.

Serve on plates garnished with the lettuce and lime slices.

The Woodward Veggyburger

What do you do when your husband is a hamburger devotee and you are inclined toward vegetarianism? Well, if you're Joanne Woodward, you invent the Veggyburger, which looks like a Newmanburger but contains no meat and can nestle in a bun just as appealingly as one of my ground chuck specials. ■ SERVES 6 TO 8

1 cup chopped onions

2 tablespoons minced garlic

1 tablespoon vegetable oil

3 tablespoons chopped fresh basil or 2 teaspoons dried

2 cups cooked brown rice

⅓ cup cashews

⅓ cup walnuts

⅓ cup almonds

⅓ cup sunflower seeds

¼ cup tamari sauce (concentrated soy sauce)

⅔ cup tahini (sesame seed paste)

In a frying pan, sauté the onions and garlic in the oil. When onions are translucent, add the basil and mix well. Add the mixture to the cooked rice.

Lightly toast nuts in frying pan and allow to cool. In a blender or food processor, grind all the nuts and sunflower seeds until coarsely ground. Add to the rice mixture with the tamari sauce and tahini. Shape into patties. To cook, brown in a nonstick pan.

Veggyburgers should be served in pita bread or burger buns with your favorite accompaniments.

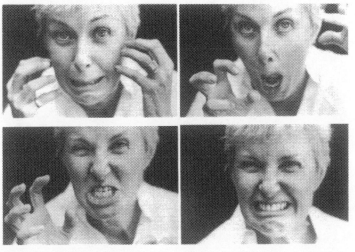

Joanne's reaction when she doesn't find a bottle of Newman's Own dressing in her cupboard

Twice-Baked Potato over Spinach, Broccoli, and Peppers

These are not the typical stratospherically high-calorie stuffed potatoes. Different and definitely worth a try, and a whole potato makes a filling main course for any hungry vegetarian. The soy milk, soy bacon, and soy cheese can all be found at any good health food store and at some better-stocked supermarkets. ■ SERVES 6

3 large Idaho potatoes, baked until soft
¾ cup low-fat sour cream
¼ cup soy milk
3 tablespoons unsalted butter
5 strips soy bacon, chopped
⅓ cup chopped chives
salt and freshly ground black pepper to taste
8 ounces soy cheese (your favorite flavor), grated

VEGETABLES

¼ cup olive oil
1 tablespoon chopped garlic

1 large red pepper, cut into julienne strips
1 cup broccoli florets
one 10-ounce package frozen chopped spinach, thawed and squeezed of liquid
¼ cup dry white wine
salt and freshly ground black pepper to taste
½ cup Newman's Own Bombolina Spaghetti Sauce or your favorite

½ cup grated soy Parmesan cheese for garnish
½ cup chopped basil for garnish

Preheat the oven to 450°F.

Let the potatoes cool until they can be handled, then cut in half and scoop out the insides. Reserve the shells.

In a saucepan, combine the potatoes with the sour cream, milk, and butter, and mash over low heat until combined. Add the bacon, chives, salt, and pepper, and stir to combine. Spoon the filling into the shells, rounding the tops nicely, and sprinkle with the cheese.

Place the stuffed halves in a 13 x 9 x 2-inch baking pan and cover loosely with foil. Bake, covered, for 15 minutes. Remove the foil and bake 5 minutes more.

While the potatoes are baking, prepare the vegetables: In a large saucepan, heat the oil over high heat until hot. Add the garlic and pepper, and cook, stirring, for 5 minutes. Add the broccoli and cook, tossing, for 4 minutes. Add the spinach, wine, salt, and pepper. Stir in the sauce, cover, lower the heat to medium, and simmer for 7 minutes.

To serve, divide the vegetables among 6 plates. Place a stuffed potato half on top and sprinkle with some of the Parmesan cheese and basil.

Nell Newman's Marinated Ginger Tofu over Crispy Browned Soba Noodles

I used to buy tofu occasionally and attempted to scramble it or eat it raw, only to be disgusted by its lack of flavor. I finally discovered that tofu is mainly a carrier for flavors. It is very rich in protein and contains no cholesterol. If you are willing to experiment, you can make anything from main courses to desserts with it.

For this dinner recipe you can use just about any vegetable you want, particularly Chinese vegetables, which require less cooking time than many Western vegetables. Delicate vegetables such as bok choy (which can be found in Asian markets and many supermarkets) and red peppers should not be simmered with the tofu but placed in the marinade before putting the dish in the oven.

Even if you have never tried tofu and are generally skeptical about new foods, I promise you will enjoy this dish! ■ SERVES 4

1 pound tofu	2 stalks celery, sliced ¼ to ½ inch thick
⅔ cup tamari sauce or regular soy sauce	3 stalks bok choy
2 teaspoons grated fresh gingerroot	1 large zucchini, sliced ½ inch thick
1 large onion, coarsely chopped	8 ounces soba noodles
½ large red pepper, coarsely chopped	3 tablespoons sesame oil

Simmer the tofu in the soy sauce with the gingerroot, onion, and the 2¼ cups of water for 1 hour. Allow to marinate for at least 1 hour or up to 5 hours.

Preheat the oven to 350°F.

Place the red pepper, celery, bok choy, and zucchini in a large, shallow, ovenproof dish and pour the tofu and marinade over them. Braise for 30 to 60 minutes, depending on how you like your tofu or how much time you have. I usually cook it until the tofu is browned and the sauce is bubbly.

While the tofu is cooking, place the soba noodles in boiling water with 1 tablespoon of sesame oil and cook until al dente. Drain and place in a nonstick pan over medium-high heat. Add the remaining 2 tablespoons of sesame oil and spread the noodles so they cover the pan evenly. Cook until darkly browned or lightly burned. To serve, spoon the tofu mixture over individual portions of the fried noodles.

Potato and Cheese Quesadillas with Green and Red Sauces

A hashed brown potato filling makes these vegetarian quesadillas a little different and mighty good. If you cook the hashed browns and combine the green sauce ahead of time, all that's left to do is assemble the tortillas and fry them—not too taxing, all in all.

■ SERVES 4

HASHED BROWN POTATOES

1 tablespoon vegetable oil
1 cup finely diced peeled Idaho potato
½ cup chopped red onion
¼ cup diced red bell pepper
¼ cup chopped scallion, green and
    white parts
salt and freshly ground black pepper to
    taste

GREEN SAUCE

4 tomatillos, husked and chopped
¼ small yellow onion, chopped
3 cloves garlic, chopped
½ small serrano or jalapeño chili
    pepper, seeded

½ cup chopped cilantro
1 tablespoon fresh lime juice
salt and freshly ground black pepper to
    taste

8 corn tortillas
12 ounces Monterey Jack cheese, sliced
1 tablespoon vegetable oil for frying

ACCOMPANIMENTS

one 11-ounce jar Newman's Own All-
    Natural Bandito Salsa or your
    favorite
1 avocado, chopped
½ cup sour cream
chopped cilantro

To make the hashed brown potatoes: Heat the oil in a medium skillet until hot. Add the potatoes and cook, tossing, for 5 minutes. Add the onion, bell pepper, scallion, salt, and pepper, and cook, turning occasionally, about 10 minutes, until the potatoes are crispy and browned.

To make the green sauce: In a blender, combine the tomatillos, onion, garlic, chili, cilantro, lime juice, salt, and pepper with ¼ cup of water until smooth. Pour into a serving bowl.

To make the quesadillas: Place ¼ of the hashed potatoes on 4 tortillas and top each with 3 ounces of the sliced cheese. Heat the vegetable oil in a large skillet until hot. Add

2 tortillas, top each with a tortilla, and cook until lightly browned on the bottom. Turn and cook until the cheese is melted and the bottom is browned. Remove, keep warm, and cook remaining tortillas in same manner.

Serve immediately, with the green sauce and a bowl of salsa on the side. Have bowls of the avocado, sour cream, and cilantro alongside for serving.

Piñata Pockets

Piñata Pockets Joan Klearman of St. Louis, Missouri, created a delicious, healthful Mexican entree that is impressive and yet easy to prepare; it was a 1993 finalist. Her festive tortilla "piñatas," baked under a zesty topping of Newman's Own All-Natural Bandito Salsa, burst with a colorful surprise of vegetables and spices. Joan donated her prize money to the English Language School in St. Louis. ■ SERVES 5

2 teaspoons salad oil
2 medium red bell peppers, chopped
1 large onion, chopped
1 tablespoon chili powder
1 teaspoon ground cumin
2 plum tomatoes, chopped
one 15- to 19-ounce can black beans, rinsed and drained
one 10-ounce package frozen corn kernels
one 4-ounce can chopped mild green chiles, drained
one 4-ounce can (drained weight) pitted ripe olives, chopped

juice of 1 lime
10 flour or corn tortillas, each 6 inches in diameter
two 11-ounce jars Newman's Own All-Natural Bandito Salsa (mild, medium, or hot) or your favorite
4 ounces low-fat Monterey Jack cheese, shredded
chopped parsley for garnish
light sour cream and sliced avocado for serving (optional)

Heat the oil over medium-high heat in a 3-quart saucepan. Add the peppers and onion, and cook until tender-crisp. Add the chili powder and cumin, and cook for 1 minute. Stir in the tomatoes, black beans, corn, chiles, olives, and lime juice, and bring to a boil. Lower the heat to medium, cover, and cook for 15 minutes to blend the flavors.

Preheat the oven to 350°F.

Spoon about ½ cup of the vegetable mixture down the center of each tortilla, then roll up the tortilla to enclose the filling. Place the tortillas, seam side down, in a 13 x 9-inch glass baking dish. Spoon the salsa over the tortillas and sprinkle the cheese over all. Bake for 20 minutes, or until the salsa is hot and the cheese is melted.

To serve, garnish the piñatas with chopped parsley and serve with sour cream and sliced avocado as accompaniments.

Pastas, Pizza, and Rice

Baked Macaroni with Lamb and Cheese ■

Rigatoni with Chicken Sausage and Artichokes ■

Cappellini with Sautéed Shrimp Caesar ■ The

Hudsucker Pasta ■ Tom Cruise's Linguine with Zesty

Red Clam Sauce ■ Shells with Red Sauce and Blue

Cheese ■ Nicole Kidman's Crispy Orechiette with

Broccoli, Pine Nuts, and Garlic ■ Fettuccine Alfredo

à la Newman ■ David Copperfield's Spicy Penne

with Fontina Cheese ■ Venezia Sauce al Mare y

Newmano ■ Gene Shalit's Spaghetti Carbonara ■

Rigatoni with Fat-Free Rosemary-Spinach Pesto ■

Lasagna Primavera ■ Italian Artichoke Pasta ■

Newman's Whitecap Pizza ▪ **Sundance Summer Risotto** ▪ **Susan Sarandon's Risotto with Scallops and Asparagus**

Baked Macaroni with Lamb and Cheese

Chances are you won't find ground lamb in the meat department of most supermarkets, which means you will have to ask the butcher to grind lamb for you; or you can use shoulder of lamb, diced, as a substitute. Like the best of made-from-scratch macaroni and cheese, this one soothes the soul. It is rich and comforting and different. ■ SERVES 6

1 pound small macaroni	one 8-ounce can evaporated milk
1 tablespoon vegetable oil	2 cups shredded sharp cheddar cheese
4 cloves garlic, chopped	½ cup shredded mozzarella cheese
1 pound ground lamb	one 4-ounce log unashed goat cheese,
one 10-ounce package frozen chopped	crumbled
spinach, thawed but not drained	salt and freshly ground black pepper to
1 cup heavy cream	taste

Preheat the oven to 450°F.

Bring a large pot of salted water to a boil. Add the macaroni and cook according to the package directions until tender but still firm.

Meanwhile, heat the oil in a large saucepan over high heat until hot. Add the garlic, lamb, and spinach, and cook, stirring, for 5 minutes, until the lamb is no longer pink. Add the cream and evaporated milk, and bring to a boil. Lower the heat to medium-high and cook the mixture about 5 minutes until it almost coats the back of a spoon. Turn the heat to low and add 1½ cups of the cheddar cheese and all the mozzarella and goat cheese, stirring until melted. Taste and season lightly with salt (the cheeses are quite salty) and more liberally with pepper.

Drain the macaroni well in a large colander, then place in a medium casserole. Add the cream sauce and toss to combine. Sprinkle the remaining ½ cup of cheddar cheese on top and bake for 7 to 10 minutes, until bubbling.

Rigatoni with Chicken Sausage and Artichokes

If you roast the peppers and make the pesto for this in advance, you have a great dish that comes together easily, at the last minute if need be. It's entirely your call on which type of sausage to use—fresh or smoked both work. Serve with a simple green salad, good bread, and a young red wine.

■ MAKES 1¼ CUPS OF PESTO ■ SERVES 6

PESTO

2 cups chopped fresh basil leaves

¼ cup pine nuts

2 cloves garlic, coarsely chopped

½ cup freshly grated Parmesan cheese

½ cup olive oil

salt and freshly ground black pepper to taste

PASTA

1 pound rigatoni pasta

1 tablespoon olive oil

3 fresh or smoked chicken sausages, sliced ¼ inch thick

4 roasted red peppers (page 137), cored, seeded, and cut into julienne strips (to yield 2 cups)

one 6-ounce jar marinated artichoke hearts, drained and coarsely chopped

salt and freshly ground black pepper to taste

¼ cup dry white wine

¾ cup Newman's Own "Say Cheese" Pasta Sauce or your favorite

1 cup freshly grated Parmesan cheese

To make the pesto: Combine the basil, pine nuts, garlic, and cheese in a blender or food processor and blend until coarsely chopped. With the machine running, add the oil slowly, blending until combined. Season with salt and pepper. Set aside.

Bring a large pot of salted water to a boil, add the rigatoni, and cook according to the package directions until firm but tender.

Meanwhile, heat the oil in a large skillet until hot. Add the fresh sausage and cook, turning the pieces, until browned on all sides. If using smoked sausage, toss the pieces in the oil just to coat. Add the pepper strips, artichoke hearts, salt, and pepper, and cook, stirring, until heated through. Add the wine and cook for 30 to 40 seconds. Add the sauce and cook, stirring, until heated through, 1 or 2 minutes. Remove the pan from the heat.

To Roast Red Bell Peppers

There are several ways to roast fresh peppers: on the grill, directly over the flame on a gas stove, or in a lightly oiled cast-iron skillet. The goal is to cook them until blackened on all sides. No matter how you choose to do it, use tongs to turn them.

When the peppers are charred—really black all over—remove them from the heat and let cool until you can handle them. Then put the peppers under running water and peel off the black. Some little bits and pieces may not want to come off, and that is fine.

Core the peppers and seed them. They can be used in salads, as part of an antipasto, or in a recipe such as Rigatoni with Chicken Sausage and Artichokes (page 136).

You can also buy roasted peppers in jars in the supermarket. The ones you roast yourself, though, have a freshness and sweetness of flavor that can't be matched.

Drain the pasta. Still off the heat, add the pasta to the hot sauce with ½ cup of the cheese and half of the pesto. Toss well and adjust the seasonings to taste. Refrigerate or freeze the remaining pesto for another use.

Serve immediately in heated bowls, with the remaining cheese on the side.

Cappellini with Sautéed Shrimp Caesar

Here is another simple, mighty fine dish that needs nothing more than a green salad and a loaf of good bread. We like it with Chianti, although a bottle of white wine would be okay, too. ■ SERVES 6

2 tablespoons olive oil

3 cloves garlic, slivered

30 medium shrimp, peeled and deveined

1 large red onion, cut into julienne strips

1 large red bell pepper, cut into julienne strips

1 cup fresh or frozen and thawed peas

1 pound cappellini pasta

¾ cup Newman's Own Caesar Dressing or your favorite

¾ cup freshly grated Parmesan cheese

salt and freshly ground black pepper to taste

Bring a large pot of salted water to a boil.

Meanwhile, heat the oil in a large skillet or sauté pan over medium-high heat until hot. Add the garlic and cook until golden. Add the shrimp and cook, tossing, until barely pink. With a slotted spoon, remove the shrimp to a plate and cover loosely. Add the onion, pepper, and peas to the skillet and cook, stirring, until the onion is softened and the pepper is tender but still crisp, about 5 minutes. Return the shrimp to the skillet and sauté briefly, stirring to combine with the vegetables and to rewarm. Be careful not to overcook. Remove from the heat and keep warm.

Add the pasta to the boiling water, stir to separate the strands, and cook according to the package directions. Drain and place in a large heated bowl. Add the shrimp sauce, dressing, and ½ cup of the cheese. Toss well and season with salt and pepper.

Serve immediately in heated bowls, with the remaining ¼ cup of cheese on the side.

The Hudsucker Pasta

Shannon Wiggs, an assistant school principal, loves creamy, tomato-based pasta sauces. She discovered that shrimp cooked together with Newman's Own Bombolina Spaghetti Sauce, Neufchâtel cheese, fresh mushrooms, and sun-dried tomatoes, served over pasta, made for a quick, flavorful, and elegant dish. A 1995 runner-up, she donated her award to Nativity House in Tacoma, Washington. ▪ SERVES 4

3 cloves garlic, crushed

2 tablespoons olive oil

8 ounces mushrooms, sliced

½ cup sun-dried tomatoes packed in oil, drained and chopped

2 cups Newman's Own Bombolina Spaghetti Sauce or your favorite

¼ cup dry red wine

1 tablespoon balsamic vinegar

¼ teaspoon crushed red pepper flakes

4 ounces Neufchâtel or cream cheese, cubed

1¼ pounds shrimp, peeled and deveined

12 ounces penne pasta

½ cup grated Parmesan cheese

¼ cup toasted pine nuts

chopped parsley for serving

In a 12-inch skillet, sauté the garlic in the olive oil over medium heat for 2 minutes. Add the mushrooms and sauté until tender. Add the tomatoes, sauce, wine, vinegar, and crushed red pepper flakes, and simmer for 7 minutes. Add the Neufchâtel cheese and stir until it melts. Add the shrimp and simmer until they turn opaque throughout, about 5 minutes.

Meanwhile, cook the penne according to the package directions, until al dente. Drain and place in a large serving bowl.

Top the pasta with the shrimp sauce. Sprinkle with the Parmesan cheese, pine nuts, and parsley, toss, and serve immediately.

Tom Cruise's Linguine with Zesty Red Clam Sauce

This is not your typical red clam sauce. You use freshly steamed clams here, served in their shells, in a light tomato sauce heady with garlic, that is peppery, too.

To crush garlic, use the same technique you do to peel it. First separate the cloves from the head. Put the flat side of a knife down on one garlic clove at a time and with your other hand smack the knife right over the clove. This should split the garlic peel with one whack. If it doesn't, try again. Remove the peels and use the cloves whole. ■ MAKES ABOUT 4½ CUPS OF SAUCE ■ SERVES 6

TOMATO SAUCE

½ cup olive oil

¼ cup cloves garlic, crushed

¼ cup capers, undrained

2 cups chopped parsley, plus ½ cup additional for garnish

2 cups chopped plum tomatoes

¾ cup fresh lemon juice

¾ cup dry white wine

½ teaspoon crushed red pepper flakes

1 teaspoon salt

1 heaping teaspoon freshly ground black pepper

PASTA

1 pound linguine

CLAMS

30 littleneck clams, scrubbed

¼ cup chopped garlic

1 cup dry white wine

1 cup vegetable broth or water

To make the tomato sauce: Heat the oil in a large saucepan until hot. Add the garlic and capers, then carefully add the parsley. Stand back because the oil may spatter. Add the tomatoes, lemon juice, wine, pepper flakes, salt, and black pepper. Cook, stirring occasionally, for 15 minutes.

Bring a large pot of salted water to a boil. Add the linguine and cook according to the package directions until firm but tender.

While the pasta is cooking, steam the clams. Place the clams in another large pot with the garlic, wine, and vegetable broth. Cover and bring to a boil over high heat, shaking the pot, until all the shells are open. Leaving the open clams in the pot, drain off all but

¼ cup of the steaming liquid and stir it into the tomato sauce. Cover the clams and keep warm while preparing the rest of the dish.

Drain the linguine and add to the tomato sauce. Cook over high heat for about 4 minutes to heat through.

Divide the pasta among 6 heated bowls. Top each serving with 5 clams and garnish with the remaining parsley.

Shells with Red Sauce and Blue Cheese This is simple, tasty, and quick. It is ready in the time it takes to cook the shells.

■ SERVES 6

1 pound small shells
2 tablespoons olive oil
4 cloves garlic, chopped
1 cup chopped fresh tomatoes
one 10-ounce package frozen peas, thawed
salt and freshly ground black pepper to taste

¾ cup crumbled good-quality blue cheese
½ cup Newman's Own Industrial Strength Venetian Spaghetti Sauce with Mushrooms or your favorite
2 tablespoons freshly grated Parmesan cheese for serving

Bring a large pot of salted water to a boil, add the pasta, and cook according to the package directions. Drain well and keep warm.

Meanwhile, make the sauce: Heat the oil in a medium sauté pan over high heat until hot. Add the garlic, tomatoes, peas, salt, and pepper, and cook, stirring occasionally, for 5 minutes. Add the drained pasta and toss until combined. Stir in the blue cheese and sauce and toss until mixed.

Divide the pasta among 6 pasta bowls or plates and sprinkle each serving with a little Parmesan cheese.

Nicole Kidman's Crispy Orechiette with Broccoli, Pine Nuts, and Garlic

This is a one-of-a-kind dish. The great appeal is the orechiette: It is meant to be crunchy. Don't jump the gun when you are cooking the pasta and take it out before it is crisp.

■ SERVES 6

1½ boxes (16 ounces each) orechiette (little ears)

¾ cup vegetable oil

2 tablespoons slivered garlic

5 cups small broccoli florets

⅓ cup dry white wine

¼ cup fresh lemon juice

salt and freshly ground black pepper to taste

3 tablespoons balsamic vinegar

6 tablespoons unsalted butter, cut in chunks and softened

½ cup toasted pine nuts

1 cup freshly grated Parmesan cheese

In a stockpot, cook the orechiette in plenty of salted boiling water until tender but firm. Drain, run under cold water, and drain well again.

Have ready 2 medium sauté pans. Heat ¼ cup of oil in each until smoking. Add the cooked orechiette carefully to the hot oil, dividing it equally. Spread the pasta out in even layers and cook for about 3 minutes, or until medium brown on the underside. Turn the pasta over and cook, without stirring, until browned on the other side. Transfer the pasta and oil to a large bowl and keep warm.

Heat the remaining ¼ cup of oil in one pan until hot. Add the garlic and broccoli, and sauté, tossing, for 5 minutes. Add the wine, lemon juice, salt, and pepper. Taste, adjust the seasonings if necessary, and cook for 3 minutes. Transfer to a large (13 × 9-inch) flameproof baking dish.

Add the browned orechiette, balsamic vinegar, butter, and pine nuts to the baking dish and toss over medium-high heat until the butter is melted. Add ½ cup of the cheese and toss to combine.

Serve the pasta in 6 heated bowls or plates, with a generous grinding of fresh black pepper on top and the remaining cheese on the side.

Fettuccine Alfredo à la Newman

Fettuccine Alfredo has never been credited with any dietary virtues, only gustatory ones—and lots of them. This rendition is slightly different: It has less butter but more cream than usual, an egg yolk (which makes up for the missing butter), and peas. If we hadn't pointed it out to you, you probably wouldn't even have known the butter wasn't there. Don't let the cream put you off. This is very good, and tomorrow is another day, as someone once said. ■ SERVES 6

1 pound fettuccine

1 teaspoon unsalted butter

1½ cups frozen baby peas, thawed

¼ cup dry white wine

juice of 1 lemon

1½ cups heavy cream

1 egg yolk

1¼ cups freshly grated Parmesan cheese

1 teaspoon salt

1 tablespoon freshly ground black pepper

chopped Italian flat-leaf parsley for garnish (optional)

Bring a large pot of salted water to a boil. Add the fettuccine and cook according to the package directions until firm but tender.

Meanwhile, melt the butter in a large saucepan over medium-high heat. Add the peas and cook for 1 minute. Add the white wine and lemon juice, and reduce the mixture by half. Add the cream and cook over high heat for 4 to 5 minutes, until it almost coats a spoon. Remove the pan from the heat and quickly whisk in the egg yolk. Add ¾ cup of the cheese, salt, and pepper, and whisk rapidly to combine well.

Drain the fettuccine, add it to the saucepan, and toss quickly, until coated.

Serve the fettuccine immediately, garnished with the parsley and with the remaining ½ cup of Parmesan cheese on the side.

David Copperfield's Spicy Penne with Fontina Cheese

If you grow your own basil, you are in luck here; you'll need a *big* bunch for this recipe. The remaining ingredients are straightforward and simple, and together they add up to a satisfying sauce. The key is in letting the fontina only partially melt. ■ SERVES 6

1 pound penne
¼ cup olive oil
1½ cups frozen and thawed peas (½ cup less than a 10-ounce package)
2 small yellow onions, cut into julienne strips
1 cup chopped basil leaves
¼ cup dry white wine

juice of 1 lemon
1½ cups Newman's Own All-Natural Diavolo Sauce or your favorite
½ teaspoon crushed red pepper flakes
8 ounces fontina cheese, grated
salt (optional)
fresh Parmesan cheese for grating at the table

Bring a large pot of salted water to a boil. Add the penne and cook according to the package directions until tender but firm. Drain well and keep warm.

Meanwhile, heat the oil in a large sauté pan over high heat until hot. Add the peas, onions, and basil leaves, and cook, stirring, for 5 minutes. Add the wine and lemon juice, and cook for 3 minutes. Add the sauce and pepper flakes and bring to a simmer, stirring, until hot. Stir in the fontina cheese and cook for barely 30 seconds, until semi-melted.

Add the penne to the sauce and toss well. Taste and add salt if needed.

Serve at once in heated bowls, sprinkled with the Parmesan cheese.

Venezia Sauce al Mare y Newmano

Newman's Own Industrial Strength Venetian Spaghetti Sauce with Mushrooms is quickly and elegantly transformed by the flavorful addition of green olives, capers, golden raisins, and pine nuts in Cheryll McDowell's 1995 finalist recipe. She initially developed this to be used over shrimp but has found that chicken is an outstanding substitute. Cheryll donated her award to Susan G. Koman Breast Cancer Research Foundation and Friends of the Cowlitz. ■ SERVES 6

1 pound vermicelli
½ teaspoon crushed red pepper flakes
1 teaspoon extra-virgin olive oil
one 26-ounce jar Newman's Own
    Industrial Strength Venetian
    Spaghetti Sauce with Mushrooms
    or your favorite
½ cup green olives

¼ cup capers
¼ cup golden raisins
¼ cup pine nuts
1 tablespoon chopped fresh basil
1 tablespoon chopped fresh parsley
1¼ pounds large shrimp, peeled and
    deveined

Cook the vermicelli according to the package directions.

Meanwhile, in a 12-inch skillet, cook the crushed red pepper flakes in the oil for 2 minutes. Add the sauce and green olives, and cook until the sauce begins to bubble, about 5 minutes.

Add the capers, raisins, pine nuts, basil, and parsley, and cook for 5 minutes.

Add the shrimp and bring the mixture to a boil. Lower the heat to medium, cover the skillet, and cook for 5 minutes, or until the shrimp turn opaque throughout. Stir ½ cup of the pasta cooking water into the sauce.

Drain the vermicelli. Serve the pasta with the shrimp sauce on top.

Gene Shalit's Spaghetti Carbonara

There is a surprise ingredient in this version of spaghetti Carbonara—fresh tomatoes. They add color and tang to what is an unspeakably indulgent dish that you have to have every now and then as a reminder of just how delicious it is. ■ SERVES 6

1 pound spaghetti
1 tablespoon olive oil
1 tablespoon chopped garlic
½ cup diced onion
2 cups chopped Roma tomatoes
1½ cups heavy cream
8 strips bacon, cooked, drained, and
    crumbled

½ teaspoon salt
½ teaspoon freshly ground black
    pepper
¾ cup freshly grated Parmesan cheese
½ cup minced Italian flat-leaf parsley
    for garnish

Bring a large pot of salted water to a boil. Add the spaghetti and cook according to the package directions until firm but tender.

Meanwhile, heat the oil in a large sauté pan over high heat until hot. Add the garlic, onion, and tomatoes, and cook, stirring, for 8 minutes. Add the cream and cook about 5 minutes to reduce it by about one quarter. Stir in the bacon, salt, and pepper until combined. Remove the pan from the heat.

Drain the pasta, add it at once to the sauce, and toss to coat. Put the pan over medium heat and add ¼ cup of the cheese. Toss until the cheese is fully blended in and the strands are well coated.

Serve at once, garnished with the parsley and with the remaining cheese on the side.

Rigatoni with Fat-Free Rosemary-Spinach Pesto

Classic Italian pesto is made with fresh basil plus oil, cheese, and nuts—quite a payload when it comes to fat. Even if the pesto we have here isn't authentic, it is a terrific sauce, especially with pasta. It is also wonderful as a spread or dip. You'll have some left over, so you can see how you like it best.

■ **MAKES ABOUT 1½ CUPS OF PESTO** ■ **SERVES 6**

ROSEMARY-SPINACH PESTO

2 cups chopped, rinsed, and patted dry
    fresh spinach leaves

2 tablespoons fresh rosemary leaves

2 tablespoons chopped garlic

2 tablespoons chopped onion

¼ cup rice wine vinegar

juice of 1 orange

salt and freshly ground black pepper to
    taste

1 pound rigatoni

¼ cup olive oil

2 tablespoons slivered garlic

1 cup asparagus pieces (3 or 4 stalks,
    depending on size, cut ½ each long)

1 cup yellow squash pieces (1 large
    squash, halved lengthwise and cut
    into ¼-inch pieces)

¼ teaspoon salt

½ teaspoon freshly ground black
    pepper

1½ cups Newman's Own "Say Cheese"
    Pasta Sauce or your favorite

½ cup freshly grated Parmesan cheese
    (optional)

To make the pesto: Combine the spinach and rosemary leaves, garlic, onion, vinegar, orange juice, salt, and pepper in a blender and blend until pureed. (Adjust the consistency by adding more orange juice to thin the pesto if desired.) If made in advance, store the pesto in the refrigerator, covered with a piece of plastic wrap directly on the surface to prevent the sauce from discoloring; it will keep for 1 week.

Bring a large pot of salted water to a boil. Add the rigatoni and cook according to the package directions until tender.

Meanwhile, heat the oil in a skillet or sauté pan until hot. Add the garlic, asparagus, squash, salt, and pepper, and sauté, stirring, for 3 minutes. Stir in the sauce and cook over medium heat, stirring, until hot and the pasta is cooked.

Drain the rigatoni and place in a large bowl. Add the vegetable sauce and toss. Add ¾ cup of the pesto and toss again.

Serve at once in wide, heated pasta bowls, sprinkled with the Parmesan cheese.

Lasagna Primavera
This is a light and beautiful lasagna. Janet Sutherland's clever method of blanching the fresh vegetables with the pasta streamlines the preparation. Janet won the 1992 grand prize for this recipe and donated the money to the Assistance League of Escondido Valley. ■ SERVES 8

one 8-ounce package lasagna noodles
3 carrots, cut into ¼-inch slices
1 cup broccoli florets
1 cup zucchini slices, cut ¼ inch thick
1 crookneck squash, cut into ¼-inch
    slices
two 10-ounce packages frozen chopped
    spinach, thawed

8 ounces ricotta cheese
one 26-ounce jar Newman's Own All-
    Natural Marinara Style Spaghetti
    Sauce with Mushrooms or your
    favorite
12 ounces shredded mozzarella cheese
½ cup grated Parmesan cheese

Preheat the oven to 400°F. Line a 15 × 10-inch baking sheet with foil.

Bring 3 quarts of water to a boil in a 6-quart saucepan over high heat. Add the lasagna noodles and cook for 5 minutes. Add the carrots and cook 2 minutes more. Add the broccoli, zucchini, and squash, and cook for 2 minutes more, or until the pasta is tender. Drain the noodles and vegetables well.

Squeeze any liquid from the spinach. Combine the spinach with the ricotta cheese.

Spread ⅓ of the sauce on the bottom of a 3-quart rectangular baking pan. Line the pan with half of the lasagna noodles. Top with half of each vegetable, half of the spinach mixture, and half of the mozzarella cheese. Pour half of the remaining sauce over the top. Continue to make layers with the remaining ingredients, ending with a layer of sauce. Sprinkle the Parmesan cheese over the sauce.

Bake the lasagna, uncovered, on the prepared baking sheet for approximately 30 minutes, or until hot in the center. Let stand for 10 minutes before serving.

The lasagna may be prepared up to 2 days in advance and kept, covered, in the refrigerator. If made in advance and chilled, bake the lasagna at 350°F for 1 hour.

Serve with Italian bread or rolls, a green salad with Newman's Own Light Italian Dressing, and red wine.

Italian Artichoke Pasta

A group effort headed by the Sunset Hill P.T.A. fund-raising chairman challenged parents to create winning recipes. They succeeded with this 1996 runner-up. Newman's Own gives high marks to Sue Kakuk, John Crow, and the Sunset Hill P.T.A. in Plymouth, Minnesota, for this recipe, which is easy to make and very impressive to serve. The award went to the Sunset Hill P.T.A. ■ SERVES 6 AS A MAIN DISH

4 teaspoons olive oil

1 whole, large, skinless, boneless chicken breast, cut into 2-inch pieces

1 pound linguine

8 ounces mushrooms, sliced

1 clove garlic, finely chopped

one 8-ounce bottle Newman's Own Olive Oil and Vinegar Dressing or your favorite

one 14-ounce can artichoke hearts, drained and cut into quarters

1 pint cherry tomatoes, cut in half

freshly grated Parmesan cheese

Heat 2 teaspoons of the oil in a 10-inch nonstick skillet over medium-high heat. Add the chicken and cook for 3 to 5 minutes, turning when needed, until tender and opaque. Remove the chicken from the skillet and keep warm.

Meanwhile, cook the linguine according to the package directions. Drain and keep warm.

In the skillet, heat the remaining 2 teaspoons of oil, add the mushrooms, and cook until their juice evaporates and they are browned. Add the garlic and cook for 1 to 2 minutes. Stir in the dressing, artichoke hearts, and cherry tomatoes. Cover and cook over medium heat for 5 minutes. Add the chicken and cook until heated through.

Divide the hot pasta among 6 plates or pasta bowls, top each serving with sauce, and sprinkle with the cheese.

Newman's Whitecap Pizza
Linda Mangen of Valrico, Florida, put a new twist on a classic pizza for her winning recipe. This 1992 finalist gave her award to the University of Tampa Scholarship Fund. ■ SERVES 4

1 pound skinless, boneless chicken
    breast
one 16-ounce bottle Newman's Olive
    Oil and Vinegar Dressing or
    Newman's Own Light Italian
    Dressing or your favorite
1 ready-to-bake pizza crust

8 ounces feta cheese, crumbled
one 4-ounce can artichoke hearts
8 ounces mozzarella cheese, shredded
4 lettuce leaves
2 beefsteak tomatoes
one 4-ounce can sliced black olives

Cut the chicken into bite-size pieces and place in a nonreactive container with half of the bottle of salad dressing. Marinate in the refrigerator for 3 to 5 hours.

Preheat the oven to 400°F.

Brush a large baking sheet with 2 tablespoons of salad dressing. Put the pizza crust on the baking sheet. Brush the top of the pizza crust with 2 tablespoons of dressing.

Drain the chicken. In a hot skillet, sauté the chicken for approximately 5 minutes, or until all the liquid has evaporated.

Sprinkle the feta over the pizza crust. Drain the artichoke hearts and squeeze out any excess moisture. Tear the artichokes into bite-size pieces. Place the chicken and artichoke hearts over the feta, covering the entire pizza. Sprinkle the mozzarella over all.

Bake the pizza for 15 to 18 minutes. Remove, let stand for 2 minutes, and cut into 8 wedges.

Serve the pizza with 4 individual bowls of salad; combine the lettuce, sliced beefsteak tomatoes, and sliced olives, then drizzle each salad with some of the remaining dressing.

Sundance Summer Risotto

Sundance Summer Risotto This is a great-looking, great-tasting risotto, made with a slight twist: The stock isn't heated before it is added to the rice. Have 6 cups of stock on hand but know that you may not need all of it—you'll probably use 5 cups at most. What is the only way to know when a risotto is ready to serve, when the rice is creamy and firm but not hard? Taste it and keep tasting it until it is right. But you should do that whenever you cook.

■ SERVES 6

RISOTTO

1 teaspoon olive oil
¼ cup finely chopped red onion
2 cups Arborio rice
1 cup dry white wine
4 to 6 cups homemade or natural (MSG-free) chicken or vegetable stock

½ cup ½-inch asparagus pieces, cut on the diagonal
½ cup chopped tomato
¾ cup fresh or frozen corn kernels
salt and freshly ground black pepper to taste
¾ cup freshly grated Parmesan cheese

To make the risotto: Heat the oil in a large saucepan over medium-high heat until hot. Add the onion, and cook, stirring, until translucent. Add the rice and stir to coat it evenly. Stir in the wine and cook for 1 or 2 minutes. Add the stock by the ladleful, stirring it slowly into the rice until fully absorbed. Keep adding the stock by the ladleful and stirring it in. The risotto is done when the mixture is creamy but the rice is firm to the bite, a total of about 20 to 25 minutes. There should be almost no liquid remaining in the pan. Do not feel obliged to use all the stock but do stir constantly.

While the risotto is cooking, heat the remaining 1 teaspoon of oil in a skillet until hot. Add the asparagus, tomato, and corn, and cook, stirring, until crisp-tender. Season with salt and pepper.

Stir the hot risotto into the vegetables and combine well. Stir in ½ cup of the cheese until blended.

Serve at once in bowls, with the remaining ¼ cup of cheese as garnish.

Susan Sarandon's Risotto with Scallops and Asparagus

This is a springtime risotto if there ever was one. If you can enlist a sous-chef or helper at the stove for the last few minutes of cooking, do so. One of you should stir the risotto; the other should attend to the bay scallops and vegetables. With attention like that to each part of the dish, there's much less likelihood of overcooking the scallops, something you don't want to do. ■ SERVES 6

RISOTTO

1 teaspoon olive oil

¼ cup finely chopped red onion

2 cups Arborio rice

1 cup dry white wine

4 to 6 cups homemade or natural (MSG-free) chicken or vegetable stock

1 teaspoon olive oil

1 tablespoon finely chopped garlic

1½ cups bay scallops

1 cup chopped tomatoes

½ cup ½-inch asparagus pieces, cut on the diagonal

salt and freshly ground black pepper to taste

¾ cup freshly grated Parmesan cheese

Make the risotto following the directions on page 154.

While you are cooking the risotto, heat the oil in a large skillet over medium-high heat until hot. Add the garlic and cook, stirring, until fragrant but not colored. Add the scallops and toss quickly with the garlic. Add the tomatoes and asparagus, and sauté the mixture, tossing until the scallops are cooked through but the vegetables are still crisp-tender, about 5 to 10 minutes. Remove the pan from the heat and season with salt and pepper.

Add the risotto to the scallops and vegetables, and stir to combine well. Taste and adjust the seasonings. Stir in ½ cup of the cheese.

Serve at once in heated bowls or soup plates, with the remaining ¼ cup of cheese on the side.

Vegetables and Side Dishes

Sautéed Beet Greens ▪ Newman's
Creamed Spinach ▪ Grilled Vegetables ▪
Caramelized East Indian Vegetables ▪ Balsamic
Eggplant and Potatoes ▪ Garlicky Mashed Potatoes ▪
Honey Mustard Mashed Potatoes ▪ Roasted Herbed
New Potatoes with Spinach ▪ Potato Salad with Two
Mustards Dressing ▪ Creamy Potato Salad ▪ Braised
Root Vegetables ▪ Yam Gratin ▪ Sandy Austin's
Brown Rice Salad ▪ Butch's Wild West Tex-Mex Salad

The dishes I concoct—in my sleep, at the racetrack, and elsewhere—usually incorporate meat, but Joanne prefers meals that use vegetables, whole grains, and natural foods. So dinner at our house is as likely to feature brown rice or tofu as beef.

While the following recipes can be served as side dishes in smaller portions, many are hearty enough to serve as entrees. Just toss a salad, slice some homemade bread, and serve.

—PAUL NEWMAN

Cross-dressing for the 1996 camp gala

Sautéed Beet Greens

Substitute well-rinsed spinach or Swiss chard here if you are unable to find beet greens. The tofu contributes a nice creaminess and makes this more of a main dish for vegetarians. If tofu is not for you, leave it out. ▨ SERVES 6

1¾ pounds beet greens
1 tablespoon olive oil
1 clove garlic, minced
3 shallots, coarsely chopped
¾ cup diced firm tofu (optional)

¼ cup dry white wine
2 tablespoons toasted sesame seeds
1 tablespoon unsalted butter
¼ teaspoon Worcestershire sauce

Stem the beet greens, rinse the leaves well, and julienne the leaves. You should have 10 cups of shredded leaves. Pat dry with paper towels.

Heat the oil in a large skillet over medium heat until hot. Add the garlic and shallots, and cook, stirring, until the shallots are just softened. Raise the heat to medium-high and add the beet greens. Sauté, tossing, until the leaves wilt, 5 to 7 minutes.

Lower the heat to medium. Add the tofu, wine, and sesame seeds, and toss gently until heated through. Stir in the butter and Worcestershire sauce.

Serve hot.

Newman's Creamed Spinach Very simple, very rich, and very, very good. ■ SERVES 4

1 pound fresh spinach

⅛ teaspoon ground nutmeg

3 ounces cream cheese, softened

½ cup heavy cream

Wash the spinach well and trim the stems. Place the spinach in a saucepan with just the water that clings to the leaves. Sprinkle with the nutmeg, cover, and steam for 2 to 3 minutes, until the leaves are wilted. Drain any excess liquid. Finely chop the spinach and return to the saucepan.

Beat the cream cheese in a small bowl until fluffy. Gradually beat in the heavy cream until blended. Stir the cream cheese mixture into the chopped spinach. Cook over medium heat, stirring frequently, until blended and creamy. Serve immediately.

Grilled Vegetables

Grilled vegetables are great with any barbecue or roast, or use them as an ingredient in green or rice salads, omelets, or even frittatas. We've made extra here, and once you have the grill going, why not? Vary the vegetables as you like. Another good choice is fresh fennel, cut into thick slices. ■ SERVES 12

½ cup olive oil, or more to taste
1 tablespoon Worcestershire sauce
1 tablespoon balsamic vinegar
Spike seasoning to taste
½ cup chopped fresh basil leaves
6 ears of corn, shucked and cut in half
1 large eggplant, cut lengthwise into
    6 slices and halved
2 large zucchini, trimmed, cut into
    thirds, and halved

2 red bell peppers, cored, seeded, and
    cut into quarters
2 green bell peppers, cored, seeded,
    and cut into quarters
3 bunches scallions, trimmed and
    halved
1 yam, peeled and thinly sliced
freshly ground black pepper to taste
Newman's Own Ranch Dressing and
    Newman's Own Caesar Dressing or
    your favorite for dipping

Preheat the grill until hot.

In a baking pan, combine the oil, Worcestershire sauce, vinegar, Spike seasoning, and basil. Add all the vegetables and toss to coat.

Grill the vegetables in a hinged grill pan about 4 inches from the heat: about 10 minutes, turning often, for the corn; 4 minutes per side for the zucchini; 3½ minutes per side for the peppers; 2½ to 3 minutes per side for the eggplant; 2 to 4 minutes per side for the yam slices; and 2 to 3 minutes, turning often, for the scallions.

Serve the vegetables on a platter. Grind plenty of fresh pepper over them. Place the dressings in bowls for dipping.

NOTE: Spike seasoning is a mixture of assorted herbs and seaweed. It can be found in most health food stores.

Caramelized East Indian Vegetables These
vegetables can be used as an accompaniment to Danny Aiello's New York Strip
Steak and His Cherokee Indian Curry AAA Steak Sauce (see page 65). Or try
them as a bed on which to steam sea bass fillets in foil, or as a vegetarian sauce
for pasta. They are four star as a topping for warm focaccia, too. ■ SERVES 6

6 carrots, peeled and cut into 1-inch
   pieces
¼ cup vegetable oil
2 small Spanish onions, cut into julienne
   strips
1 small eggplant (12 ounces), unpeeled
   but diced

¼ cup rice wine vinegar
¼ cup sugar
2 tablespoons unsalted butter
1 tablespoon ground cumin
1 teaspoon salt
1 teaspoon freshly ground black
   pepper

Parboil the carrots in a large saucepan of boiling water about 10 minutes, until just soft
when tested with a fork. Drain, run under cold water to stop the cooking, and pat the
carrots dry with paper towels. Cover and refrigerate until ready to use.

Heat the oil in a large skillet or sauté pan over medium-high heat until hot. Add the
onions and eggplant, and cook, tossing, for 8 minutes, until softened. Add the carrots
and cook, tossing, for 5 minutes. Pour in the vinegar and cook for 2 minutes. Stir in the
sugar until dissolved. The pan juices will thicken and look shiny. Add the butter, cumin,
salt, and pepper, and stir until the butter is melted and all the vegetables are coated.

Serve warm.

Balsamic Eggplant and Potatoes
For a really delightful mix of tastes and colors, pair this with Herbed Salmon Fillets in Foil (page 107). Serve the vegetables alongside or, better still, use them as a bed for the salmon. Any leftovers are great on hard rolls or crusty French bread.

■ **SERVES 6**

¾ cup high-quality balsamic vinegar

¼ cup honey mustard

3 bunches scallions, both green and white parts, trimmed and thinly sliced

half of an 8-ounce jar sun-dried tomatoes packed in oil, drained and cut into julienne strips

5 Yukon Gold potatoes (about 2½ pounds), diced and reserved in cold water to cover

¼ cup vegetable oil

1 large eggplant (about 1¼ pounds), unpeeled but diced

salt and freshly ground black pepper to taste

In a bowl, whisk the balsamic vinegar into the mustard. Stir in the scallions and sun-dried tomatoes, and set side.

Pat the potatoes dry with paper towels.

Heat 2 tablespoons of the oil in a large skillet or sauté pan over high heat until hot. Add the potatoes and cook, tossing gently, for 8 minutes. In another skillet, heat the remaining 2 tablespoons of oil over high heat until hot. Add the eggplant and cook, tossing occasionally, for 6 minutes. Add the eggplant to the potatoes. Pour in the balsamic vinegar mixture, toss to combine well, and cook over medium heat for about 2 minutes, until heated through. Season with lots of salt and pepper.

Serve hot or at room temperature.

Garlicky Mashed Potatoes

These mashed potatoes are fantastic when served with Garlic-Herb Marinated Halibut with Lemon Sauce (page 118) as well as with roasted meat or poultry or other types of fish. What they lack in butter is made up for by the heavy cream. If you're watching your fat grams, you can use milk instead. They'll still be tasty, but not as decadently satisfying.

Use an old-fashioned handheld masher. The hardware store variety that looks something like a short-handled hoe is the way to go. ■ SERVES 6

5 large Idaho potatoes
½ cup chopped fresh basil leaves
¼ cup chopped garlic

2 to 2¼ cups heavy cream or low-fat milk, if you insist
salt and freshly ground black pepper to taste

Peel and quarter the potatoes, place in a large saucepan, and cover with cold water. Boil gently for 15 to 20 minutes, until soft when tested with a fork. Drain well and return to the saucepan.

Mash the potatoes with a potato masher, then stir in the basil and garlic. Add the cream slowly, stirring it in. Use enough to make the right consistency, creamy and fluffy. Season with salt and pepper.

Serve at once or spoon into a bowl, cover tightly with plastic wrap, and set the bowl in a pan of hot water. Keep warm by setting the pan over a very low flame until serving time.

Honey Mustard Mashed Potatoes
These mashed potatoes were created to be served with Sarah Jessica Parker's Grilled Shrimp with Vodka-Lime Sauce (page 119) for a super combination of sweet and sour flavors. They are also good with Lamb Chops in Minty Marinade (page 74) or Tony Randall's Grilled Veal Chop with Bourbon–Cracked Black Pepper Sauce (page 78). When you come right down to it, meat of almost any kind with mashed potatoes is a hard combo to improve on. For our convictions on potato mashers—a more important point than you might think when it comes to this singular dish—see the previous recipe on page 164. ■ SERVES 6

5 large Idaho potatoes
2 cups heavy cream
1/3 cup honey mustard
4 tablespoons unsalted butter, cut into
    chunks and softened

1½ tablespoons freshly ground black
    pepper
salt to taste

Peel, quarter, boil, and drain the potatoes as directed in Garlicky Mashed Potatoes (page 164).

Return the potatoes to the saucepan and add 1 cup of the cream, mustard, and butter. Mash with a potato masher, gradually adding more cream until you have the texture you like best. Add the pepper and fluff with a fork. Season with salt and serve at once or hold in a water bath according to the directions on page 164.

Roasted Herbed New Potatoes with Spinach

These are mighty fine as is but become unforgettable when served with Matthew Broderick's Grilled T-bone Steak with Sweet Onion Marmalade and Campfire Mustard Sauce (page 64). You'll need fresh tarragon, and if you can't find it, substitute another fresh herb (not dried) such as rosemary or basil. It's the combination of colors and fresh flavors that really sets these potatoes apart.

■ SERVES 6

12 small new red potatoes, scrubbed
¼ cup olive oil
1 tablespoon chopped fresh tarragon
salt and freshly ground black pepper to taste

10 ounces fresh spinach, washed, stems removed, patted dry, and coarsely chopped

Preheat the oven to 450°F.

Place the potatoes in a large saucepan and cover with cold water. Boil gently over medium-high heat until soft, about 20 minutes. Drain, run under cold water to stop the cooking, and halve the potatoes.

Arrange in a single layer in a large glass baking dish. Add the oil, tarragon, salt, and pepper. Toss gently to coat. Roast for 15 minutes.

Spread the spinach over the potatoes in an even layer and pour ½ cup of water into the dish. Roast 5 minutes more.

Serve at once.

Potato Salad with Two Mustards Dressing

If you're looking for something socially acceptable or even well bred to serve with Whoopi Goldberg's Big Bad Ass Beef Ribs (page 68), this is it. It's also very good to take on picnics because, unlike a lot of potato salad we've had, this is mayo and oil free. ■ SERVES 6

6 medium red potatoes, preferably Red
    Rose, scrubbed but not peeled
¼ cup seasoned rice wine vinegar
2 tablespoons honey mustard
1 tablespoon Dijon mustard

2 tablespoons capers, drained
2 stalks celery, finely chopped
salt and freshly ground black pepper to
    taste

Place the potatoes in a large saucepan and cover with cold water. Boil gently over medium-high heat for 15 to 20 minutes, until just fork-tender. Drain, run under cold water to stop the cooking, and cut into 8 pieces each.

In a large bowl, whisk together the vinegar and mustards. Stir in the capers. Add the potatoes and celery, and toss. Season with salt and plenty of fresh pepper.

Creamy Potato Salad

The dressing on this potato salad is tangy and tart, and goes particularly well with Spice-Rubbed Roasted Turkey Breast (page 100) for a summertime meal. If you don't have shallots, you can use sliced scallion or finely chopped red onion instead. ■ SERVES 6

16 small new red potatoes, scrubbed	½ teaspoon salt
½ cup sour cream	1 teaspoon freshly ground black
¼ cup Dijon mustard	pepper
juice of 1 lemon	4 shallots, finely chopped

Place the potatoes in a large saucepan and cover with cold water. Boil gently over medium for about 20 minutes, until just fork-tender. Drain, run under cold water to stop the cooking, and halve or quarter according to their size.

In a large salad bowl, whisk together the sour cream, mustard, lemon juice, salt, and pepper. Add the potatoes and shallots, and toss gently to combine. Serve immediately. If made ahead, cover and refrigerate; remove and let come to room temperature before serving.

Braised Root Vegetables

Braised Root Vegetables Three root vegetables—potatoes, parsnips, and carrots—are featured in this braise that is terrific served alongside Tony Randall's Grilled Veal Chop with Bourbon–Cracked Black Pepper Sauce (page 78). A word of caution: Don't confuse parsnips with turnips. Parsnips are carrot-shaped but creamy in color. Turnips are white, too, or yellow, in which case they are rutabagas. We like parsnips; turnips, we're not so sure about. We know we want parsnips here and think you will, too. ■ SERVES 6

4 medium baking potatoes, peeled, diced, and placed in cold water to cover

2 tablespoons olive oil

2 large parsnips, peeled and diced

2 large carrots, peeled and diced

salt and freshly ground black pepper to taste

chopped fresh parsley for garnish

Pat the potatoes dry with paper towels.

Heat the oil in a large skillet or sauté pan over high heat until hot. Add the potatoes and cook, tossing, for 8 minutes. Add the parsnips, carrots, salt, pepper, and ½ cup of water. Cover the pan and lower the heat to medium-high. Braise the vegetables for 15 minutes, until just fork-tender.

Serve with plenty of fresh parsley on top.

Yam Gratin

Yam Gratin If you want to go all out, serve this grand but so very comforting gratin with Danny Aiello's New York Strip Steak and his Cherokee Indian Curry AAA Steak Sauce (page 65) and Caramelized East Indian Vegetables (page 162) for a special dinner.

You can also serve this to good effect with something as simple as roast chicken. ■ SERVES 6

3 large yams, peeled and sliced paper-thin	2 cups grated fat-free Monterey Jack or cheddar cheese, or a combination of both
3 tablespoons chopped garlic	½ cup freshly grated Parmesan cheese
2 tablespoons chopped fresh marjoram or 1 tablespoon dried	1 cup heavy cream
salt and freshly ground black pepper to taste	4 tablespoons unsalted butter at room temperature

Preheat the oven to 400°F. Lightly butter a 13 × 9-inch gratin dish.

Arrange ⅓ of the yam slices in overlapping rows on the bottom of the prepared dish. Sprinkle on ⅓ of the garlic and marjoram, and season with salt and pepper. Sprinkle with ⅓ of the Monterey Jack and Parmesan cheeses, then pour ⅓ of the cream over all. Dot with ⅓ of the butter. Press the slices down slightly with a metal spatula.

Make 2 more layers with the remaining ingredients, ending with a dusting of Parmesan cheese.

Cover the dish with foil and bake for 50 minutes. Remove the foil and bake 5 to 10 minutes more to brown the top lightly.

Serve the gratin hot, either cut into squares or spooned from the dish.

Sandy Austin's Brown Rice Salad
Joanne is particularly fond of this dish because of the whole-grain base. It goes beautifully with Caroline's Southern-Fried Chicken (page 84). ■ SERVES 6 TO 10

DRESSING

½ ounce fresh gingerroot, peeled

1½ tablespoons cider vinegar

1½ tablespoons brown sugar

2 tablespoons champagne vinegar

½ cup olive oil

½ cup vegetable oil

⅛ teaspoon ground nutmeg

salt to taste

1 teaspoon freshly ground black
  pepper

2 tablespoons toasted and ground
  coriander seeds

1 pound brown rice

juice and zest of 1 orange

3 scallions, thinly sliced crosswise

1½ pounds red or green seedless
  grapes, stemmed

5 ounces whole almonds, toasted

Blend the dressing ingredients in a food processor or blender until emulsified.

In a large saucepan, boil the rice in salted water until tender. Drain immediately. Place the hot rice in a large bowl. Stir in the dressing, orange juice and zest, and scallions. Let cool.

Adjust the seasonings to taste and add more oil if needed. Fold in the grapes and almonds, and toss well.

Last spring my husband and I were enjoying the beach on Siesta Key (Sarasota, Florida). A group of young musicians had the apartment below us for the week. . . .

By the third day they were very red and very miserable. . . . Reaching for my trusty bottle of Paul Newman Vinegar and Oil, I said, "Try rubbing this all over!" They did, and it worked—honest! They even wrote a song about it: "Rub it on, cool it off."

SINCERELY YOURS,
A.

Butch's Wild West Tex-Mex Salad

To showcase the flavors of the Southwest, Cindy Kovar created a colorful and flavorful salad. This perfect make-ahead side dish walked away with the 1996 grand prize. Chipotle chiles in adobo sauce add big flavor—Texas style! They are available in the Spanish food section in most grocery stores or in specialty food stores. Cindy donated her award to the 100 Pennies Scholarship Drive.

■ SERVES 6 AS A MAIN DISH OR 12 AS AN ACCOMPANIMENT

DRESSING

1 cup Newman's Own Olive Oil and
    Vinegar Dressing or your favorite
¼ cup red wine vinegar
3 tablespoons chipotle chiles in adobo
    sauce, chopped
juice of 1 large lime (about
    2 tablespoons)
1 tablespoon ground cumin
2 teaspoons salt

SALAD

3 cans (15½ to 19 ounces each) black
    beans, rinsed and drained
4 cans (15½ to 16 ounces each) whole
    kernel corn, drained
3 cups cooked white rice
¾ cup finely chopped red onion
½ cup finely chopped green onions,
    including the tops
½ cup chopped cilantro

2 cups coarsely chopped tomatoes
lime wedges and cilantro sprigs for
    garnish

To make the dressing: Mix all the ingredients together well in a bowl.

To make the salad: Mix all the salad ingredients in a large bowl.

Add the dressing to the salad, toss, cover, and place in the refrigerator for at least 1 hour or up to 1 day.

Before serving the salad, add the chopped tomatoes and garnish with the lime wedges and cilantro sprigs.

Breads and Snacks

Jalapeño Spoon Bread ▪ **Cornmeal Squares with Salsa** ▪ **Nell Newman's Whole Wheat Raisin Scones** ▪ **Joanne's Zucchini Bread** ▪ **Nell's Sesame Loaves** ▪ **Joanne's Cereal** ▪ **Newman's Munchies** ▪ **Paul's Picture Show Popcorn Crunch** ▪ **"Pops" Newman's Coffee-Toffee Macadamia Crunch**

Jalapeño Spoon Bread

This Southwest-style spoon bread is tailor-made for serving with Harry Belafonte's Pork, Apple, and Yam Salad (page 73). If you don't have a large cast-iron skillet, bake it in an 11 x 9-inch baking pan. Be sure to serve it warm. ■ SERVES 6

1½ cups yellow cornmeal

⅓ cup flour

3 cups low-fat or regular milk

1 stick (8 tablespoons) unsalted butter, melted

½ teaspoon salt

4 egg yolks

2 teaspoons baking powder

⅓ cup frozen corn kernels, thawed

¼ cup julienned basil leaves

1 jalapeño or serrano chili, seeded and diced

1 tablespoon freshly ground black pepper

2 egg whites at room temperature

Preheat the oven to 350°F. Generously butter a 12-inch cast-iron skillet.

Sift the cornmeal and flour together in a bowl.

In a medium saucepan, bring 2 cups of the milk just to a boil. Add the cornmeal mixture gradually, whisking it in vigorously. Stir in the butter and salt. Cook over medium heat for 2 minutes, then transfer to a bowl and let cool to room temperature.

Beat the egg yolks with an electric mixer until they form a ribbon when the beater is lifted. Stir into the cooled cornmeal mixture with the baking powder and the remaining 1 cup of milk. Stir in the corn, basil, chili, and black pepper, and combine well.

Beat the egg whites with the electric mixer and clean beaters until stiff but not dry. Fold into the cornmeal batter until fully incorporated.

Scrape the batter into the prepared skillet and level the top. Bake for 30 to 40 minutes, or until a knife inserted in the center comes out clean.

Serve warm, in wedges.

Dear Sir:

Recently after reading about some of the research on hot spicy foods . . . I decided to try some of your salsa sauce. I now eat your salsa several times per week and have experienced a clearing of the lung congestion that has troubled me for years. . . . It was amazing the results after a few days of eating cheese and crackers topped with your salsa—my left lung is now as clear as a bell. . . .

SINCERELY YOURS,
J.B.

Cornmeal Squares with Salsa

Salsa, mild, medium, or hot, makes a surefire topping for these grilled cornmeal squares with chiles, cheese, and cilantro. Staying in the southwestern mode, serve as a bread with chili. These are also good with soup and/or a main-course salad.

■ MAKES 15 SQUARES ■ SERVES 4 TO 6

1 cup yellow cornmeal
1 teaspoon chili powder
1 teaspoon salt
1 cup grated Monterey Jack cheese
one 4-ounce can green chiles, drained, chopped, and patted dry

¼ cup chopped cilantro
6 tablespoons vegetable oil
one 11-ounce jar Newman's Own All-Natural Bandito Salsa or your favorite

Oil a 15 × 10 × ½-inch baking pan.

Combine the cornmeal and chili powder in a small bowl.

In a large saucepan, bring 4 cups of water and the salt to a boil over medium heat. Sprinkle the cornmeal mixture, ¼ cup at a time, into the water, whisking constantly. Cook, stirring constantly with a wooden spoon, until thickened, about 10 minutes. Stir in the cheese, chiles, and cilantro. Spread the batter evenly in the prepared baking pan and refrigerate until cooled completely.

Cut the cold corn bread into 15 squares, each 3 by 3¼ inches. In a large nonstick skillet, heat 2 tablespoons of the oil over medium-high heat. Place 5 squares in the skillet and cook, turning once, until golden brown, about 8 to 10 minutes. Remove to a plate.

Cook the remaining squares, in batches of 5, in the same manner with the remaining oil.

Serve the corn bread squares warm with the salsa as a topping.

Nell Newman's Whole Wheat Raisin Scones

While in England one spring, I managed to get a recipe for this traditional teatime treat from a family friend. Her scones were made with white flour and sugar, which I have changed to whole wheat and honey as a matter of personal preference. They can be made either way or somewhere in between; white flour makes lighter scones. This is best served at teatime with heavy doses of butter and jam. ■ MAKES 8 TO 12

1 stick (8 tablespoons) unsalted butter	⅓ cup milk
¼ cup honey	3 teaspoons baking soda
2 cups whole wheat flour	¼ cup raisins

Preheat the oven to 350°F. Grease a cookie sheet well, then flour it lightly.

In a medium bowl, combine the butter, honey, and flour with your hands until it resembles coarse meal. Stir in the milk, baking soda, and raisins until well mixed and a doughy ball forms.

Lightly flour the work surface and the top of the dough ball. Roll the dough evenly in all directions until it is ¾ to 1 inch thick. Using the rim of a glass or a cookie cutter with a diameter of 2 to 2½ inches, cut out individual scones and place on the prepared cookie sheet. Bake for 20 to 30 minutes, or until browned on top.

The scones can be served hot out of the oven or cold.

Joanne's Zucchini Bread
This is good for breakfast, as an accompaniment to a bowl of soup for lunch, or with a cup of coffee or tea as a snack. ■ MAKES 2 LOAVES

3 cups flour	3 eggs
1 teaspoon baking soda	1 cup sugar
1 teaspoon baking powder	1 cup vegetable oil
1 teaspoon ground cinnamon	1 teaspoon vanilla extract
1 teaspoon salt	2 cups grated zucchini (about 2 large)

Preheat the oven to 350°F. Grease well 2 loaf pans, each 8½ × 4½ × 2½ inches.

Sift together the flour, baking soda, baking powder, cinnamon, and salt.

In a large bowl, beat the eggs until foamy. Add the sugar, oil, vanilla extract, and dry ingredients, a little at a time. The batter will be thick. Add the zucchini; the mixture will be gummy.

Pour the batter into the prepared loaf pans and bake for 1 hour. Check after 50 minutes. If a toothpick comes out clean, the bread is done.

Great served warm or cold. The loaves may be frozen.

Nell's Sesame Loaves

My family is quite fond of this wonderful recipe. Consequently, it doesn't last long in our household, especially since it goes so well with soups, salads, or sandwiches such as Caroline Murphy's Tuna Salad (page 115). I would love to lie and say it is my original creation, but I must give credit where credit is due. This recipe was given to me by family friend, and professional cook, Cary Bell of Bar Harbor, Maine.

■ MAKES 2 LOAVES

1 cup boiling water	1 teaspoon sugar or honey
1 cup quick-cooking oats	3½ cups whole wheat flour
1 cup unhulled sesame seeds	1 teaspoon salt
1½ cups warm water	1 handful cornmeal
1 teaspoon dry yeast	

In a bowl, mix together the boiling water, oats, and sesame seeds. Let cool.

In a large bowl, combine the warm water, yeast, and sugar. Put the bowl in a warm place. When the yeast mixture is bubbly (5 to 15 minutes), add the flour, salt, and sesame mixture, and work until the dough forms a ball. (This may require a bit more flour.)

Flour the work surface as well as your hands and the dough. Transfer the dough to the floured surface and knead well for 10 to 15 minutes. Allow to rise for 45 minutes.

While the dough is rising, preheat the oven to 350°F. Grease a long, shallow baking pan or baking sheet and sprinkle it with the cornmeal.

Knead the dough again and shape it into 2 long loaves. Place the loaves in the prepared pan and bake for 30 to 50 minutes, until golden brown and hollow-sounding when tapped on the bottom with a wooden spoon or your fingers.

Joanne's Cereal

Joanne's culinary repertoire is limited, but she makes up in quality what she lacks in quantity. Her breakfast cereal is the best way for anyone to start the day, and it would certainly become a Newman's Own product if it weren't for the complicated process required to create it. It is best to make a large batch of the cereal, which can then be kept in the refrigerator for several weeks. You will need to bake this in batches; the recipe will fill 3 to 4 cookie sheets. ■ MAKES LOTS

1¼ cups vegetable oil
2 pounds honey
1 pound oats
2 pounds almonds
1 pound sunflower seeds

½ cup sesame seeds
1 cup chopped cashews
1 cup chopped walnuts
4 cups wheat germ, roasted

Preheat the oven to 325°F.

Mix the oil and honey together with 1½ cups of water. Mix together the dry ingredients. Combine all. Spread thinly on nonstick cookie sheets. Bake and keep turning until golden brown, about 20 to 30 minutes. Cool and keep in tins.

Newman's Munchies

Mary Jane Bennett used a triple play of pretzels, popcorn, and Caesar dressing teamed with mixed nuts and spices to create a savory snack. Prepare the recipe ahead. Store in airtight containers to take to your next sporting event. Mary Jane, a 1996 runner-up, donated her award to the San Diego chapter of the Achievement Rewards for College Scientists. ■ MAKES ABOUT 11 CUPS

2 cups Newman's Own Second Generation Organic Pretzel Sticks or your favorite, broken in half

2 cups whole nuts (dry-roasted unsalted cashews, macadamia nuts, pecans, or walnuts; peanuts are too small)

3 tablespoons Newman's Own Caesar Dressing or your favorite

½ teaspoon dried basil leaves

½ teaspoon dried oregano leaves

4 tablespoons grated Parmesan cheese

5 cups popped Newman's Own All-Natural Butter Flavor Oldstyle Picture Show Microwave Popcorn or your favorite, prepared according to the package directions

Preheat the oven to 300°F.

Place the pretzels and nuts in a 13 × 9-inch metal baking pan. Combine the dressing, basil, and oregano, and pour over the pretzels and nuts. Sprinkle 2 tablespoons of the cheese over all and mix to coat. Bake for 20 to 30 minutes, stirring once.

Pour half of the popcorn into a large bowl and sprinkle with 1 tablespoon of the cheese. Pour the remaining popcorn into the bowl and sprinkle with the remaining tablespoon of cheese. Add the baked pretzels and nuts, mix, and serve.

Dear Mr. Newman:

My 92-year-old dad likes popcorn but had to give it up because of the hulls getting under his dentures. I gave him a handful of your popcorn, and the first bite was followed by "Hey, that melts in your mouth." Took out his dentures and showed me—clean as a whistle.

THANKS,
W.S.

Paul's Picture Show Popcorn Crunch

This sweet and nutty snack is the creation of Jane Skvarca, a 1994 finalist. Her award was donated to the Day Nursery and the Assistance League of Antelope Valley.

■ MAKES ABOUT 13 CUPS

1 cup whole almonds	½ cup margarine
1 cup pecan halves	½ cup unsalted butter
1 cup cashews or walnuts	1⅓ cups sugar
1 bag Newman's Own Oldstyle Picture Show Microwave Popcorn (about 10 cups) or your favorite	¼ cup light corn syrup
	1 tablespoon pure vanilla extract

Preheat the oven to 300°F. Coat a large heatproof mixing bowl (16 cups or larger) and a 15 × 10-inch baking pan with margarine or nonstick cooking spray.

In another 15 × 10-inch baking pan, combine the almonds, pecans, and cashews, and toast for 20 minutes, stirring occasionally. Remove the pan from the oven and cool the nuts to room temperature.

Pop the popcorn following the package directions. Pour the popcorn into the prepared bowl. Add the nuts and mix well.

Melt the margarine and butter in a heavy 2-quart saucepan over medium heat. Add the sugar, corn syrup, and ¼ cup of water. Mix well and stir often. Continue to cook over medium-high heat until it reaches 275°F on a candy thermometer. Remove the pan from the heat and slowly stir in the vanilla extract. (Stir carefully because the vanilla extract will spatter when added to the hot syrup.)

Pour the hot syrup over the popcorn-nut mixture and mix until evenly coated. Immediately pour the popcorn into the prepared baking pan. Let cool for 1 hour. Break into pieces and store in an airtight container.

"Pops" Newman's Coffee-Toffee Macadamia Crunch

For Bob Gadsby, a love for popcorn as a child developed into an art form as a bachelor. Even though his wife is now queen of the kitchen, popcorn is one area where he reigns supreme. His 1996 prize-winning recipe combines popcorn with rich, buttery macadamia nuts and just a hint of coffee. Bob donated his award to the Boundary County Library and the Volunteer Fire Department. ■ **MAKES ABOUT 13 CUPS**

One 3½-ounce bag Newman's Own All-Natural Flavor Oldstyle Picture Show Microwave Popcorn (about 10 cups) or your favorite

2 cups coarsely chopped macadamia nuts

1½ sticks (12 tablespoons) unsalted butter or margarine

1 cup sugar

½ cup packed light brown sugar

¼ cup coffee-flavored liqueur or strong coffee

¼ cup light corn syrup

2 teaspoons vanilla extract

Butter a large roasting pan.

Pop the popcorn according to the package directions. Pour into the prepared pan and add the macadamia nuts. Toss to mix.

In a 2-quart saucepan, combine the butter, sugar, brown sugar, liqueur, and corn syrup, and bring to a boil over medium heat, stirring constantly. Continue cooking and stirring until the mixture reaches 290°F on a candy thermometer. Remove the pan from the heat and stir in the vanilla extract. Pour over the popcorn mixture and stir until evenly coated.

Cool until firm and break into pieces.

Store in an airtight container.

Desserts

Lemonade Torte for a Long Hot Summer ▪ Sockarooni Orange Kiss-Me Cake ▪ Tropical Coconut Tapioca Pudding ▪ Julia Roberts's Fresh Peach Crisp ▪ Fresh Fruits with Sour Cream Sauce ▪ Dried Cranberry and Apple Caramel Custard ▪ Raspberry Napoleons with Lemon Whipped Cream ▪ Melanie Griffith's Macadamia, Chocolate Chip, and Peanut Butter Mini-Turnovers ▪ Cy Coleman's Potstickers with Cream Cheese and Strawberry Filling ▪ Almond Fruit Pudding

The good thing about excesses is that you can't get too much of them.

—STOLEN FROM AN UNKNOWN POET BY BANDITO NEWMAN, 1985

Lemonade Torte for a Long Hot Summer

The inspiration to create this 1995 finalist recipe derived from the love of Marta Rallis-Lagreco's family for a particular chocolate torte. Marta donated her prize money to the Guide Dog Institute of America, the Gray Panthers, and HART Muttmatchers. ■ SERVES 8

¾ cup blanched almonds

1½ cups sugar

1½ cups whole wheat bread crumbs

¼ teaspoon baking powder

¼ teaspoon ground cinnamon

1 tablespoon grated lemon peel

6 large egg whites

1 cup Newman's Own Old-Fashioned Roadside Virgin Lemonade or your favorite

2 tablespoons confectioners' sugar

Preheat the oven to 350°F. Butter and flour a 9-inch springform pan.

In a food processor, grind the almonds with 1 cup of the sugar. In a medium bowl, mix the ground almond mixture with the bread crumbs, baking powder, cinnamon, and lemon peel.

In a large bowl, beat the egg whites and the remaining ½ cup of sugar with an electric mixer on high speed until stiff peaks form. Gently fold the crumb mixture into the beaten egg whites. Pour the mixture into the prepared springform pan and bake on the lower oven rack for 1 hour.

Put the lemonade in a saucepan over medium-high heat and cook for 10 minutes, until reduced by half.

Remove the torte from the oven. Pour the reduced lemonade gradually over the top of the hot torte. Let the torte stand in the pan on a wire rack until cool.

To serve, remove the sides of the springform pan and dust the top of the torte with the confectioners' sugar.

Sockarooni Orange Kiss-Me Cake

No one will ever guess the secret ingredient in this sweet and tangy cake, which secured a 1997 runner-up prize for Kim Landhuis. Kim donated her award to the Fort Dodge Public Library and the Fort Dodge United Way. ■ SERVES 12

2 large eggs

1 cup Newman's Own Sockarooni Spaghetti Sauce or your favorite

¾ cup freshly squeezed orange juice

½ cup vegetable oil

3 cups flour

1½ cups sugar

2 teaspoons pumpkin pie spice

1½ teaspoons baking powder

1½ teaspoons baking soda

1½ cups golden raisins

1 cup chopped almonds

FROSTING

6 ounces low-fat cream cheese, softened

2 tablespoons unsalted butter or margarine, softened

4 tablespoons freshly squeezed orange juice

½ teaspoon grated orange peel

1 pound confectioners' sugar

3 maraschino cherries, halved

18 almond slices

Preheat the oven to 350°F. Grease a 10-inch Bundt pan.

In a large bowl, beat the eggs until combined and add the sauce, orange juice, and oil. Mix well.

In a large bowl, combine the flour, sugar, pumpkin pie spice, baking powder, and baking soda. Beat the mixture slowly into the egg mixture. Stir in the raisins and almonds. Pour the batter into the prepared pan and bake for 40 to 50 minutes, or until a toothpick inserted in the center comes out clean. Cool the cake on a rack for 15 minutes, then remove from the pan and cool completely.

To make the frosting: In a large bowl, beat the cream cheese together with the butter, orange juice, and orange peel. Add the confectioners' sugar gradually, beating until smooth.

Spread the frosting on the cake. On the top, make 6 flower garnishes by surrounding each cherry half with 3 almond slices.

Tropical Coconut Tapioca Pudding

This is a new spin on tapioca pudding, made here with coconut milk and topped with a fresh fruit and yogurt sauce. Tapioca comes in different sizes; you want the small pearl variety. ■ **MAKES ABOUT 2 CUPS OF TOPPING** ■ **SERVES 6**

TAPIOCA

¾ cup small pearl tapioca

1¾ cups unsweetened coconut milk

1 cup milk

⅓ cup sugar

1 egg, lightly beaten

1 teaspoon vanilla extract

TOPPING

½ cup fresh blueberries

½ cup fresh raspberries

½ cup finely chopped fresh pineapple

1 medium banana, thinly sliced

¼ cup packed dark brown sugar

6 ounces vanilla yogurt

To make the tapioca: In a medium saucepan, combine the tapioca, coconut milk, milk, sugar, and egg over medium heat, stirring to dissolve the sugar. Bring to a boil and simmer, stirring constantly, for 30 minutes, or until the tapioca pearls are soft. Remove the pan from the heat and stir in the vanilla extract. Pour the tapioca into a shallow bowl. Place plastic wrap directly on the surface of the tapioca (to prevent a skin from forming) and let cool.

To make the topping: Place all the ingredients in a bowl and stir gently to combine. Cover and refrigerate until serving time.

Serve the tapioca with a generous amount of topping.

Julia Roberts's Fresh Peach Crisp

What sets this crisp apart is its topping: It is crusty and wonderful, and there is lots of it. If unpeeled peaches bother you, peel them. Serve this for dessert, of course, and also for breakfast. ■ SERVES 6

7 ripe but firm medium peaches, unpeeled, pitted, and coarsely chopped
¼ cup fresh lemon juice
¼ cup Scotch whisky
¼ cup sugar
¼ cup packed dark brown sugar
4 tablespoons unsalted butter

TOPPING

2½ cups flour
½ cup packed dark brown sugar
1 teaspoon ground cinnamon
3 sticks (24 tablespoons) unsalted butter, melted

softened frozen vanilla yogurt as an accompaniment

Preheat the oven to 350°F. Butter a 13 × 9 × 2-inch baking dish.

In a large bowl, toss the peaches together with the lemon juice. Add the whisky, sugar, and brown sugar, and combine well. Spread the mixture on the bottom of the baking dish and dot with small pieces of the butter.

To make the topping: In a bowl, stir together the flour, brown sugar, and cinnamon until combined. Add the butter gradually, stirring it in to form a crumbly mixture. Sprinkle it evenly over the peaches. Even though the topping should be evenly distributed, you want a rustic, pebbly look to the top.

Cover the dish with foil and bake for 40 minutes. Uncover and bake 5 to 10 minutes more to brown the top.

Let cool slightly, then serve warm in bowls, topped with scoops of frozen yogurt.

Fresh Fruits with Sour Cream Sauce

You don't have to use lots of this sauce to get its full marvelous effect. Assorted fresh berries are a natural with it, too. Or spoon a little of it over pound cake.

If you're looking for something really special, make the Raspberry Napoleons on page 196, and instead of dusting the plates for serving with confectioners' sugar, spoon a small pool of this sauce on the bottom of each plate, then place a Napoleon in the center. ■ SERVES 6

3½ cups sliced fresh fruits, such as
    banana, mango, papaya, and kiwi
1½ cups sour cream
⅓ cup packed dark brown sugar

juice of 1 lemon
1 teaspoon finely chopped fresh mint
    plus mint sprigs for garnish
    (optional)

Keep the fruit chilled until ready to serve.

In a bowl, combine the sour cream, brown sugar, lemon juice, and mint, and stir together until the sugar is dissolved. Pour the sauce into a serving bowl, cover, and chill until serving time.

Serve the fruit garnished with the mint sprigs and pass the sour cream sauce as a topping. Serve with crisp cookies.

Dear Sirs:

I am writing you this letter in regard to Newman's Own Virgin Lemonade. I am an auctioneer and on occasion while working my throat will get dry and have phlegm in it and makes me get hoarse. When the above happens and I get hoarse, nothing else will cut this phlegm and dryness except this Virgin Lemonade—it cuts through and cleans up my hoarseness. You should put it on the bottle—cuts through phlegm.

THANK YOU VERY MUCH,
L.E.

Dried Cranberry and Apple Caramel Custard

Most custards are made with heavy cream or milk mixed together with eggs; this unusual version uses lemonade in place of the dairy.

■ SERVES 6

CARAMEL

¾ cup sugar

3½ tablespoons water

APPLES

5 tablespoons unsalted butter

8 cups peeled and sliced tart apples (about 4 or 5 large)

¼ cup Newman's Own Old-Fashioned Roadside Virgin Lemonade

⅓ cup sugar

½ teaspoon ground cinnamon

½ cup dried cranberries

APPLE CUSTARD

4 eggs

¼ cup Newman's Own Old-Fashioned Roadside Virgin Lemonade or your favorite

2 tablespoons Grand Marnier (optional)

confectioner's sugar for garnish

To make the caramel: In a small, heavy saucepan, swirl the sugar and water together over medium heat until the sugar has dissolved and the liquid is clear. Bring the mixture to a boil and with a brush dipped in cold water constantly brush down the sugar crystals that form on the sides of the pan. Cook, without stirring, until the sugar syrup turns caramel brown in color. Immediately pour the hot syrup very carefully into a 6-cup ovenproof mold and turn it to film the bottom and sides.

To prepare the apples: In a large, heavy skillet, melt the butter over medium heat. Add the apple slices and toss until coated with the butter. Add the lemonade, sugar, cinnamon, and cranberries, and stir to combine. Cover the pan and cook the apples about 5 minutes, until soft but still holding their shape. Remove the pan from the heat and let cool.

Preheat the oven to 350°F.

To make the custard: In a large bowl, beat the eggs together with the lemonade and Grand Marnier. Fold in the apple slices and any cooking juices from the pan. Turn the mixture into the caramelized ovenproof mold.

Place the mold in a larger baking pan and pour hot water into the baking pan to come about halfway up the sides of the dish. Bake in the water bath for about 1½ hours, or until the custard shrinks slightly away from the sides. Remove from the oven. Take the mold out of the baking pan and let stand for 15 minutes. Unmold onto a serving plate.

Sprinkle the confectioners' sugar over the top and serve hot.

Raspberry Napoleons with Lemon Whipped Cream

Classic Napoleons are notoriously difficult to make, but frozen puff pastry and a whipped cream filling make all the difference here. These luscious pastries cannot be assembled too far in advance, though—no more than thirty minutes before serving time. You want to keep all the textures intact.

If these are not luxurious enough (and they are), there's a way to make them even more so: Serve in a pool of the brown sugar sour cream sauce on page 192. ■ SERVES 6

3 sheets (two 17¼-ounce packages) frozen puff pastry, thawed according to the package directions (reserve the remaining sheet for another use)	1 tablespoon confectioners' sugar plus additional for garnish
	½ teaspoon lemon extract
	freshly grated zest of 1 lemon
	three ½-pint packages raspberries
1½ cups cold heavy cream	6 mint sprigs for garnish

Preheat the oven to 450°F. Have ready 4 heavy-duty cookie sheets. Line 3 of them with parchment paper.

Working with 1 sheet of puff pastry at a time, spread the pastry sheet evenly over 1 of the cookie sheets. With a sharp knife, cut it in sixths, and cover with a lined cookie sheet. Spread a second sheet of pastry over that cookie sheet, cut it into sixths, and cover with the third cookie sheet. Top with the remaining sheet of pastry, cut it into sixths, and top with the last cookie sheet. Transfer the stacked cookie sheets to the oven and bake for 15 to 20 minutes. Carefully lift up the top cookie sheet to check the color of the pastry. It should be deep golden brown. If not, return the stack to the oven. Check every 5 minutes until the pastry is golden brown. Remove the stack from the oven, remove the top cookie sheet, and let the pastry cool.

In a large chilled bowl, beat the cream, sugar, and lemon extract with an electric mixer until soft peaks form. It should not be stiff but should fall softly from the beater in mounds. Stir in the zest. Cover and chill until it is time to assemble the dessert.

To assemble the Napoleons: Dust 6 dessert plates generously with confectioners' sugar. Place a piece of pastry on 1 plate and top with about ⅓ cup of whipped cream. Top with a small handful of berries and another piece of pastry. Add another layer of whipped cream and raspberries, and end with a third piece of pastry.

Make 5 more Napoleons with the remaining ingredients in the same way.

To serve, dust the tops of the Napoleons with confectioners' sugar and garnish each with a mint sprig. Serve immediately. The pastry is at its very best still flaky and crisp.

Melanie Griffith's Macadamia, Chocolate Chip, and Peanut Butter Mini-Turnovers

Macadamia nuts make the peanut butter filling in these turnovers unforgettable. It is a little like having a mini-candy bar wrapped in a puff pastry case. When you feel the urge coming on for these, there's an easy solution: Prepare a full batch, then freeze some of them. They freeze beautifully, we are glad to say.

■ MAKES 32 MINI-TURNOVERS

2 cups smooth peanut butter at room temperature
½ cup milk chocolate chips
1 cup toasted and chopped macadamia nuts
2 sheets (one 17¼-ounce package) frozen puff pastry, thawed according to the package directions

1 egg, lightly beaten
confectioners' sugar for garnish (optional)
mint sprigs for garnish (optional)
vanilla ice cream as an accompaniment

Preheat the oven to 425°F.

In a bowl, stir together the peanut butter, chocolate chips, and macadamia nuts until well combined.

Work with 1 sheet of puff pastry at a time. Lightly flour a work surface. Lay 1 sheet of puff pastry on the surface and gently roll it out in all directions to thin it slightly. With a sharp knife, cut the sheet into quarters, then cut each quarter into quarters, making 16 pieces total.

Center 1 teaspoon of the filling on each piece of pastry. Fold the pastry on the diagonal to form a triangle. Press the open edges of the pastry closed. (At this point the turnovers can be frozen. Arrange in layers, separated by sheets of waxed paper, in a freezer container.) Brush the top of the turnover with the beaten egg and place on a baking sheet.

Make more mini-turnovers with the remaining ingredients in the same manner and brush with the beaten egg.

Bake for 15 minutes. If the turnovers are frozen, preheat the oven to 475°F. Bake the pastries on the baking sheet for 5 minutes. Lower the heat to 400°F and bake for 15 minutes.

Serve at once, dusted with confectioners' sugar and garnished with a mint sprig, with the ice cream.

Cy Coleman's Potstickers with Cream Cheese and Strawberry Filling

Serve these dessert potstickers warm and the tropical fruit salsa well chilled.

Use either gyoza or wonton wrappers to make these. You'll have leftover wrappers; freeze them airtight because you'll want to make these again.

■ **MAKES ABOUT 2¼ CUPS OF SALSA AND 36 POTSTICKERS**

FILLING

2 cups sliced strawberries
½ cup sugar
¼ cup fresh lemon juice
1 tablespoon Grand Marnier
8 ounces whipped cream cheese

SALSA

¾ cup chopped strawberries
¾ cup chopped papaya
¾ cup chopped mango
¼ cup julienned mint leaves
2 tablespoons fresh orange juice

1 tablespoon kirsch
1 tablespoon sugar

one 12-ounce package gyoza wrappers
or wonton skins
cornstarch for baking sheet
vegetable oil for cooking

softened frozen vanilla yogurt
confectioners' sugar for garnish
(optional)
fresh mint sprigs for garnish

To make the filling: In an enamel or other nonreactive saucepan, combine the strawberries, sugar, lemon juice, and Grand Marnier. Cook over medium heat, stirring every now and then, until the liquid is evaporated, about 5 minutes. Let cool completely, then stir into the cream cheese until blended.

To make the salsa: Stir the fruit, mint leaves, orange juice, kirsch, sugar, and 2 tablespoons of water together in a bowl. Cover and refrigerate until needed.

Sprinkle a cookie sheet with cornstarch. Preheat the oven to 250°F.

Make one potsticker at a time by placing ½ teaspoon of the filling in the middle of the wrapper. Brush the edges of the wrapper with water and fold over, making either half moons or rectangles. Press the edges together to seal. (A small amount of the filling may seep out of the sides; wipe off with a damp paper towel.) Brush the filled potstickers very lightly with cornstarch and place in a single layer on the prepared cookie sheet, leaving space between them. The cornstarch helps to keep the wrappers from sticking. (The potstickers can be frozen at this point. Arrange in layers, separated by sheets of wax paper, in foil freezer containers.)

Heat ½ teaspoon of oil in a cast-iron skillet until hot. Cook in batches of 6 over medium heat, 1½ minutes per side, until golden brown. Turn and cook 1½ minutes on the other side, until golden brown. Remove to a baking sheet and keep warm in the preheated oven.

To serve, divide the salsa among 6 dessert plates, spreading it to the edges. Put 6 warm potstickers per plate in a circle on the salsa, leaving the center of the circle open. Place a scoop of yogurt in the middle. Sprinkle with confectioners' sugar and garnish with the mint sprigs.

Cy Coleman at the 1995 camp gala

Almond Fruit Pudding

Almond Fruit Pudding Try this with all the fruits suggested below, or with only one or two of them. Either way, it is an especially good dessert for winter, warming but not heavy. If you want to dress it up a bit, scatter on the top a few fresh mint sprigs and dried berries that you've soaked in kirsch. ■ SERVES 4 TO 6

8 ounces dried fruit such as cherries, blueberries, blackberries, and cranberries

1 cup sugar

¾ cup Newman's Own Old-Fashioned Roadside Virgin Lemonade or your favorite

5 eggs

1 cup ground blanched almonds

½ teaspoon almond extract

Preheat the oven to 350°F.

In a saucepan, simmer the dried fruit with ⅓ cup of the sugar and the lemonade until the fruit is tender and the liquid is nearly absorbed, about 4 minutes. Drain if necessary. Place the fruit in a 6- to 8-cup soufflé dish.

In a large bowl, beat the eggs until thick and lemon-colored. Gradually beat in the remaining ⅔ cup of sugar, 1 tablespoon at a time. Fold in the almonds and almond extract. Pour the mixture over the fruit in the soufflé dish and bake for 45 to 50 minutes, or until set.

Serve hot.

Mr. Newman:

    Last night my girlfriend treated me to a fabulous meal. It was quick and easy and quite good. . . .

    During dinner my girlfriend mentioned you were a movie star. I would be interested to know what you've made. If you act as well as you cook, your movies would be worth watching.

KEEP UP THE GOOD WORK,

M.

P.S. Are any of your movies in VCR?

What I like is when life wiggles its hips and throws me a surprise. All the experts said we couldn't produce these foods without chemical preservatives; they said we couldn't use fresh garlic and onions; they said we had to advertise; they said no business in the world could give away 100 percent of its profits. Well, we didn't listen to any of 'em, and just look at us. I feel that spreading our products around is spreading the gospel, and I'll stay at it as long as I enjoy it—and, as of now, I'm having a fine time.

—PAUL NEWMAN

Index

in the Woodward veggy-
burger, 125
Cassidy's chicken curry, 96
cataplana, Martha Stewart's
chicken, 85
cauliflower and Parmesan soup
with essence of lemon, Nell
Newman's, 46
cereal, Joanne's, 181
cheddar cheese:
in baked macaroni with lamb
and cheese, 135
in Nathan Lane's south-of-
the-border zucchini soup,
42–43
puffs with salsa cream filling,
32–33
in yam gratin, 170
cheese:
baked macaroni with lamb
and, 135
and potato quesadillas with
green and red sauces,
130–31
puffs with salsa cream filling,
32–33
soy, in twice-baked potato
over spinach, broccoli, and
peppers, 126–27
see also specific cheeses
Cherokee Indian curry AAA
steak sauce, Danny Aiello's
New York strip steak and,
65
chicken, 82–96
braised, with "Say Cheese"
pasta sauce, mushrooms,
and walnuts, 92–93
Caroline's southern-fried, 84
Cassidy kebabs and the Sundance orzo pilaf, 86–87
cataplana, Martha Stewart's,
85
curry, Cassidy's, 96

grilled paillards with grilled
ratatouille and romaine
hearts, 82
in hotch potch, 90
in incredible Cobb salad,
98–99
Ismail Merchant's yogurt (*dahi
murgh*), 89
lemon mustard, 83
marinara, Hotch's, 91
in Newman's whitecap pizza,
153
with orange salsa butter, 80
oregano afloat in the diavolo
drowning pool, Greek, 88
salad, grilled cumin, 94–95
sausages, rigatoni with artichokes and, 136–37
soup, Nell Newman's, 40–41
in towering inferno Creole
posole, 52–53
chili:
Robert Redford's lamb, with
black beans, 56
vegetarian black bean, 57
chocolate chip, macadamia, and
peanut butter mini-
turnovers, Melanie Grif-
fith's, 198–99
choux pastry, in cheese puffs
with salsa cream filling,
32–33
cioppino, Joanne Woodward's,
122
clam(s):
in Joanne Woodward's cioppino, 122
juice, in Blaze's shrimp and
sausage Creole, 123
sauce, zesty red, Tom Cruise's
linguine with, 140–41
Cobb salad, incredible, 98–99
coconut tapioca pudding, tropical, 190

cod, in Joanne Woodward's cioppino, 122
coffee-toffee macadamia crunch,
"Pops" Newman's, 185
Cool Hand Luke's brunch burrito, 124
corn:
in beef stew with potatoes and
pesto, 54–55
in Butch's wild west Tex-Mex
salad, 173
in grilled vegetables, 161
in Judge Roy's zesty white
bean bisque, 50
in piñata pockets, 132
in Sundance summer risotto,
154
in vegetarian black bean chili,
57
Cornish game hens, kiss of the
Mediterranean, 97
cornmeal:
in jalapeño spoon bread, 175
squares with salsa, 57, 177
crab, in Franklin County,
Florida's own frankly fantastic seafood gumbo, 51
cranberry, dried, and apple
caramel custard, 194–95
cream cheese:
in frosting, 189
in the Hudsucker pasta, 139
in Newman's creamed
spinach, 160
salsa filling, cheese puffs with,
32–33
and strawberry filling, Cy
Coleman's potstickers with,
200–201
Creole-style dishes:
Blaze's shrimp and sausage,
123
posole, towering inferno,
52–53

salsa (*cont.*)
  steak in a sack, Sundance's, 66–67
  see also Newman's Own All-Natural Bandito Salsa
sandwiches:
  Caroline Murphy's tuna salad, 115, 180
  Newmanburger, 69
  Woodward veggyburger, 125
Sandy Austin's brown rice salad, 171
Sarah Jessica Parker's grilled shrimp with vodka-lime sauce, 119, 165
sauces:
  bourbon-cracked black pepper, Tony Randall's grilled veal chop with, 78–79, 165, 169
  Butch's BBQ, *see* Butch's BBQ sauce
  campfire mustard, Matthew Broderick's grilled T-bone steak with sweet onion marmalade and, 64, 166
  Cherokee Indian curry AAA, Danny Aiello's New York strip steak and, 65
  green and red, potato and cheese quesadillas with, 130–31
  Joanne's hollandaise, *see* hollandaise, Joanne's
  lemon, garlic-herb marinated halibut with, 118, 164
  port wine, Hud's molasses-grilled pork with, 70–71
  "Say Cheese" pasta, braised chicken with mushrooms, walnuts and, 92–93
  sour cream, fresh fruits with, 192

vodka-lime, Sarah Jessica Parker's grilled shrimp with, 119, 165
yogurt-dill, Holly Hunter's zucchini pancakes with smoked salmon and, 34–35
see also pesto; red sauce; *specific Newman's Own sauces*
sausage:
  chicken, rigatoni with artichokes and, 136–37
  in Cool Hand Luke's brunch burrito, 124
  and shrimp Creole, Blaze's, 123
  in towering inferno Creole posole, 52–53
sautéed beet greens, 159
scallop(s):
  in Franklin County, Florida's own frankly fantastic seafood gumbo, 51
  grilled, with avocado cream and salsa, 36
  and shrimp salad with Shanghai citrus dressing, 28–29
  Susan Sarandon's risotto with asparagus and, 155
  with tangerines, piquant, 121
scones, Nell Newman's whole wheat raisin, 178
scrod:
  in Franklin County, Florida's own frankly fantastic seafood gumbo, 51
  Italian baked, 105
  à la Newman, dilled fillets of, 104
sea bass fillets, steamed with caramelized East Indian vegetables, 162
seafood:
  gumbo, Franklin County, Florida's own frankly fantastic, 51

loaves, diavolo, 116–17
see also specific seafood
sesame:
  loaves, Nell's, 115, 180
  noodles and shrimp, tasty Thai, 120
  seeds, in Joanne's cereal, 181
Shanghai citrus dressing, scallop and shrimp salad with, 28–29
shells with red sauce and blue cheese, 142
shrimp:
  Caesar, cappellini with sautéed, 138
  in diavolo seafood loaves, 116–17
  in Franklin County, Florida's own frankly fantastic seafood gumbo, 51
  in the Hudsucker pasta, 139
  Sarah Jessica Parker's grilled, with vodka-lime sauce, 119, 165
  and sausage Creole, Blaze's, 123
  and scallop salad with Shanghai citrus dressing, 28–29
  and sesame noodles, tasty Thai, 120
  in Venezia sauce al mare y Newmano, 147
snacks, 174, 181–85
  Joanne's cereal, 181
  Newman's munchies, 182
  Paul's picture show popcorn crunch, 184
  "Pops" Newman's coffee-toffee macadamia crunch, 185
soba noodles, crispy browned, Nell Newman's marinated ginger tofu over, 128–29
Sockarooni orange kiss-me cake, 189

Metric Equivalencies

Liquid and Dry Measure Equivalencies

CUSTOMARY	METRIC
¼ teaspoon	1.25 milliliters
½ teaspoon	2.5 milliliters
1 teaspoon	5 milliliters
1 tablespoon	15 milliliters
1 fluid ounce	30 milliliters
¼ cup	60 milliliters
⅓ cup	80 milliliters
½ cup	120 milliliters
1 cup	240 milliliters
1 pint (2 cups)	480 milliliters
1 quart (4 cups, 32 ounces)	960 milliliters (.96 liters)
1 gallon (4 quarts)	3.84 liters
1 ounce (by weight)	28 grams
¼ pound (4 ounces)	114 grams
1 pound (16 ounces)	454 grams
2.2 pounds	1 kilogram (1,000 grams)

Oven Temperature Equivalencies

DESCRIPTION	FAHRENHEIT	CELSIUS
Cool	200	90
Very slow	250	120
Slow	300–325	150–160
Moderately slow	325–350	160–180
Moderate	350–375	180–190
Moderately hot	375–400	190–200
Hot	400–450	200–230
Very hot	450–500	230–260

About the Authors

Paul Newman is probably best known for his spectacularly successful food conglomerate. In addition to giving the profits to charity, he also ran Frank Sinatra out of the spaghetti sauce business. On the downside, the spaghetti sauce is outgrossing his films.

He did graduate from Kenyon College magna cum lager and in the process begat a laundry business, which was the only student-run enterprise on Main Street. Yale University later awarded him an honorary Doctorate of Humane Letters for unknown reasons.

He has won four Sports Car Club of America national championships and is listed in the *Guinness Book of World Records* as the oldest driver (seventy) to win a professionally sanctioned race (the twenty-four-hour of Daytona, 1995).

He is married to the best actress on the planet, was number nineteen on Nixon's enemy list, and purely by accident has done fifty-one films and four Broadway plays.

He is generally considered by professionals to be the worst fisherman on the East Coast.

A. E. Hotchner has written twelve books and six plays, and in one way or another food has found its way into all of them. In *Papa Hemingway*, which was published in twenty-six languages in thirty-eight countries, there are vivid descriptions of memorable meals with Hemingway and dishes that Hemingway particularly liked. Of course, some of the dishes, like Hemingway's peanut butter on rye with a thick slice of Bermuda onion on top for breakfast, may not set you to licking your chops, but some of the other Hemingway-inspired dishes—such as the Hotch Potch (page 90)—definitely will.

Hotch has graphically described meals in some of his novels, most recently in *Louisiana Purchase*. In an earlier book, *King of the Hill*, Hotch depicted the summer of his life when he was twelve and there was no food on the table; to assuage his hunger he sometimes cut food ads from magazines and ate them. His dishes in this book demonstrate how far up the gourmet ladder he has climbed.